ELIZABETH WOODSON

LIVE FREE

A STUDY OF GALATIANS

Lifeway Press®
Brentwood, Tennessee

Published by Lifeway Press® • © 2025 Elizabeth Woodson

ISBN: 978-1-4300-9501-9
Item: 005847566
Dewey decimal classification: 227.4
Subject heading: BIBLE. N.T. GALATIANS--STUDY AND TEACHING \ CHRISTIAN LIFE \ FREEDOM

To order additional copies of this resource, write Lifeway Resources Customer Service; 200 Powell Place, Suite 100; Brentwood, TN 37027-7707; FAX order to 615.251.5933; call toll-free 800.458.2772; email orderentry@lifeway.com; or order online at lifeway.com.

Printed in the United States of America

Lifeway Resources
200 Powell Place, Suite 100
Brentwood, TN 37027-7707

Author represented by Erik Wolgemuth of Wolgemuth & Wilson

Cover design by: Micah Kandros

EDITORIAL TEAM, LIFEWAY WOMEN BIBLE STUDIES

Andrea Lennon
Director,
Lifeway Women

Tina Boesch
Manager

Chelsea Waack
Production Leader

Laura Magness
Content Editor

Sarah Kilgore
Production Editor

Lauren Ervin
Art Director

Shiloh Stufflebeam
Graphic Designer

TABLE OF CONTENTS

ABOUT *the* AUTHOR

ELIZABETH WOODSON is a Bible teacher and author who is passionate about equipping believers to understand the rich theological truths of Scripture. She loves helping people internalize their faith and connect it practically to everyday life.

She is a contributing author for *World on Fire*, and the author of *From Beginning to Forever* and *Embrace Your Life: How to Find Joy When the Life You Have Is Not the Life You Hoped For*. Elizabeth is also a graduate of Dallas Theological Seminary with a Masters in Christian Education and regularly serves as a teacher for Lifeway Women Academy.

HOW TO USE THIS STUDY

This Bible study book is designed to be used in a specific way, with the days of personal study walking you through the three-step study process of observation, interpretation, and application. However, the homework will also prepare you for two other essential components of this study: small group discussion and video teaching.

Our study of the Bible happens best in community. You will likely have questions as you walk through the workbook. Your time in community with me through the video teachings and/or with your small group will help resolve those questions for you.

In light of this, below are my recommendations for how to best use this study:

GROUP STUDY

Step 1: Complete the homework.

Step 2: Discuss the homework questions with your small group. I have noted some of the questions that will work well for group discussion, and these can be found on the "Group Discussion" page at the end of each session.*

Step 3: Watch the video teaching. Turn to the last page of this book for information on how to stream the teaching videos.

INDIVIDUAL STUDY

Step 1: Complete the homework.

Step 2: Watch the corresponding video teaching. Turn to the last page of this book for information on how to stream the teaching videos.

*LEADING A GROUP?

An extended leader guide PDF is available for free download at **lifeway.com/livefree.** The leader guide offers several tips and helps along with discussion guides for each session.

FOREWORD

Welcome to *Live Free: A Study of Galatians*. This study is designed to help you learn how to study the Bible. Many of us approach our study of the Bible with the primary purpose of finding truth to help us live well. And this is not a bad goal. But while the Bible was written *for us*, it was not originally written *to us*.

Each time we open our Bible, we are entering a conversation that is already in progress. These conversations are words written by the biblical authors to groups of people who lived in a different time and culture than us. The biblical authors also had a specific message they desired to communicate to their audience. So, before we look to see what the text means for us, we need to learn what the text meant to its original audience. This study you're holding in your hands was designed to teach you a process that will help you read Scripture in this way.

The process I encourage for Bible study is called the Inductive Bible Study Method, an approach that looks at the text first for observation, next for interpretation, and finally for application.[1] This process invites us to slowly walk through the text by asking three critical questions:

1. Observation asks, "What does it say?"

2. Interpretation asks, "What does it mean?"

3. Application asks, "How does it apply to my life?"

The order in which we ask these questions matters. Unfortunately, we tend to rush too quickly to application, skipping observation and interpretation. When we do this, we run the risk of developing application points that might sound good but aren't faithful to the original meaning of the text. We also rob ourselves of the opportunity to grow in our Bible study skills—to become good students of Scripture we must trust the process, which includes developing the tenacity to keep going when it gets hard.

At some point in time, all of us have come across a passage of Scripture that was confusing or difficult to understand. In this moment our first response is usually to find a commentary or look at the study notes in our Bibles. While this seems to be a helpful response, it rushes us out of a very important part of our learning process—applying our own minds to the text. Even though our lack of understanding can make us uncomfortable, this discomfort is often the place where learning happens. As we take the time to wrestle with the text on our own, rather than look for quick answers, our ability to read the Bible well grows!

For this reason, as you walk through this study I encourage you to refrain from using commentaries until after you have finished the homework and listened to the video teaching. Then, feel free to use them to answer any remaining questions you might have!

The following commentaries on Galatians are trustworthy and informed my study and writing of this book:

- *Galatians for You* by Tim Keller

- *Galatians (The Story of God Bible Commentary)* by Nijay Gupta

- *Exalting Jesus in Galatians* by David Platt

Keep in mind, commentaries don't only come in the form of books. Other types of commentaries include videos, the notes in your study Bibles, online articles, podcasts, and/or sermons from trustworthy sources. These resources can be very helpful, but when used prematurely they will stunt the growth of your personal Bible study muscles.

The ultimate goal of Bible study is to grow in our knowledge of and love for God. This growth is not merely an accumulation of knowledge for knowledge's sake; we need to apply what we learn about God to our lives. Knowing God more changes us. For this reason, at the end of each week's homework we will be challenged to meditate on what we have learned about God in that week's portion of the text and then identify at least one way we can live differently based on what we've learned. These two small steps are simple but powerful and will cause your relationship with God and others to be forever changed.

A WORD *from* THE AUTHOR

When people ask me to share my favorite books of the Bible, I usually mention one written by the apostle Paul. I resonate with his passion for ministry and appreciate the clarity and directness with which he communicated. He was a man deeply acquainted with the nuances of culture and could contextualize the gospel without losing the core of its message. He also understood the distractions, false gospels, and idols that constantly vie for our attention and heart affections. I believe that in each of the thirteen letters Paul wrote in the New Testament, he always invites us to choose the better way—the way of Christ.

This theme of choosing the better way rises to the top of his letter to the church at Galatia. In my glorified imagination, I see Paul writing this letter with great fervency after learning how the Galatian believers were being led astray by the false gospel of legalism. With each word he writes, Paul fights to ensure that nothing stands between the Galatian believers and the freedom they have in Christ, for it is this freedom that fuels both their eternal salvation and the abundant life they experience daily. The same holds true for us today. When we are freed from the power of sin, we are simultaneously freed to experience the *shalom* (wholeness and peace) that God designed us to enjoy.

As you read Paul's words, I hope you see his love for God's people shine through, even in the moments when his words are sharp and spicy! More importantly, as Paul slowly and methodically defends the truth of the gospel, I hope you are overwhelmed in all the best ways by God's love for you and the intentionality of His plan of redemption. You are deeply loved by a God who, through Christ, overcame what you could not, restoring your relationship with Him so that you can live free—both now and for eternity.

You are deeply loved
by a God who, through
Christ, overcame what you
could not, restoring your
relationship with Him so
that you can live free—both
now and for eternity.

INTRODUCTION

The book of Galatians is a small part of a big story, a story that includes all sixty-six books of the Bible. From Genesis to Revelation, every word, event, and character is interconnected and points to an overarching message about God's redemption of humanity through Jesus Christ.

This larger story, also known as a metanarrative, provides the framework we need to interpret the rest of Scripture. If we study a part of the Bible without considering the big picture, we risk incorrect or incomplete interpretation of a passage. We miss the broader themes that run throughout the text. We fail to see the significance of the cultural, historical, and literary context. And worst of all, we end up using the Bible to justify our own beliefs or opinions rather than allowing it to shape our thinking and transform our lives.

So, before we zoom in on the message of Galatians, let's zoom out to make sure we understand the story of the Bible.

ZOOM OUT
THE STORY OF THE BIBLE

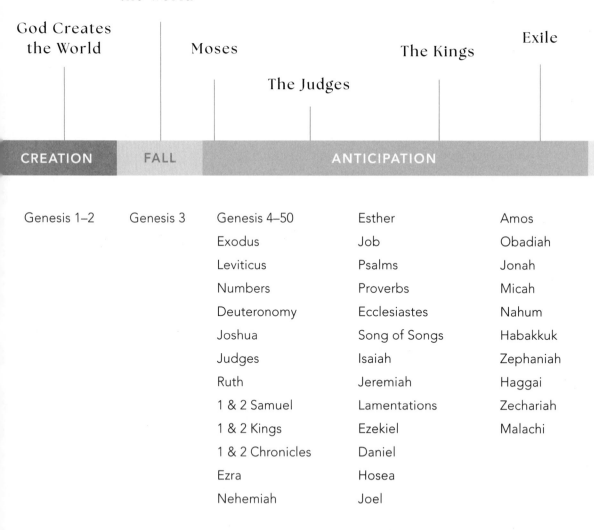

Sin Enters
the World

God Creates
the World

Moses

The Judges

The Kings

Exile

CREATION	FALL	ANTICIPATION		
Genesis 1–2	Genesis 3	Genesis 4–50	Esther	Amos
		Exodus	Job	Obadiah
		Leviticus	Psalms	Jonah
		Numbers	Proverbs	Micah
		Deuteronomy	Ecclesiastes	Nahum
		Joshua	Song of Songs	Habakkuk
		Judges	Isaiah	Zephaniah
		Ruth	Jeremiah	Haggai
		1 & 2 Samuel	Lamentations	Zechariah
		1 & 2 Kings	Ezekiel	Malachi
		1 & 2 Chronicles	Daniel	
		Ezra	Hosea	
		Nehemiah	Joel	

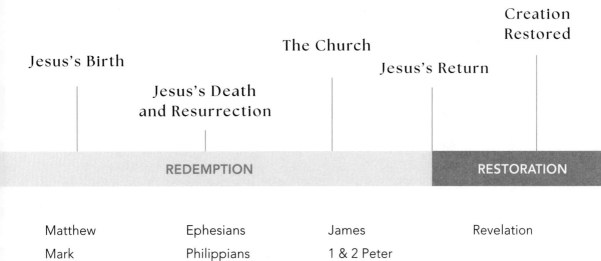

Jesus's Birth

Jesus's Death
and Resurrection

The Church

Jesus's Return

Creation
Restored

REDEMPTION   RESTORATION

Matthew	Ephesians	James	Revelation
Mark	Philippians	1 & 2 Peter	
Luke	Colossians	1, 2, & 3 John	
John	1 & 2 Thessalonians	Jude	
Acts	1 & 2 Timothy		
Romans	Titus		
1 & 2 Corinthians	Philemon		
Galatians	Hebrews		

CHAPTER 1: CREATION

GENESIS 1–2

From the very first sentence in Genesis, we are told that God created the world. Out of nothing, all of creation came into being by His power. From the overflow of His love, God created nature, animals, and humans—male and female. Unlike the rest of creation, God created humanity in His image. As image bearers, we were designed to be God's representatives, reflecting His glory to the world. We were also given the responsibility to cultivate the earth, building a beautiful world for the benefit of humanity and God's glory.

In the beginning everything was perfect. Then something changed.

CHAPTER 2: FALL

GENESIS 3

Eve got a visit from Satan in the form of a talking serpent. He suggested that she shouldn't follow the rules God had given her but should do what she thought was best. In rebellion, Adam and Eve rejected God's rule over them and decided to live as their own gods. With this one decision they unleashed sin into the world, and suddenly, what God created perfect was broken. But in His grace, God promised to fix all that sin destroyed.

CHAPTER 3: ANTICIPATION

GENESIS 4–MALACHI

As the story unfolded, God's restoration plan was accomplished through a series of promises, called covenants. God started with a man named Abraham, making a covenant to bless his family and to use his family to bless the world. After hundreds of years, Abraham's descendants, the nation of Israel, became enslaved. Remembering His covenant, God used a man named Moses to set them free. But He also made another covenant with Israel.

Through Moses, God committed to be Israel's King, and they committed to follow Him. God gave them the law, showing Israel how to live as His people by loving Him and loving others. But Israel had one problem—they kept choosing their way over God's way. In the midst of it all, God made another covenant with Israel through a king named David. God promised to raise up a King that would rule forever, perfectly leading Israel to love God and love others.

But Israel continued to persist in a sinful lifestyle. God used prophets to call them to repent, but they didn't listen. So, in love, God punished Israel by sending them into exile. During this exile, He made one last covenant with them, promising to provide a permanent solution to their sin. He would save not only Israel but all of humanity through a future King who would lead them to live in God's way.

God eventually released Israel from exile, but they continued to struggle with sin. Israel needed God's promised Savior and, for hundreds of years, they waited, anticipating His arrival.

CHAPTER 4: REDEMPTION

MATTHEW–JUDE

One night, a virgin girl named Mary gave birth to a baby named Jesus. This child was the Messianic King God had promised Israel. At thirty, Jesus began His ministry by telling Israel He is God, their promised King and Savior. Along the way, He gathered a few disciples to follow and learn from Him. With them by His side, Jesus told Israel about the kingdom of God, teaching them that kingdom living involves rejecting selfishness, embracing God's sovereign authority, and prioritizing the flourishing of all humanity.

Jesus told Israel that salvation from sin and entrance into the kingdom comes through Him alone. Some accepted His message. Most didn't, and they ended up killing Him because of it. But three days after Jesus's death, He was resurrected from the grave—conquering sin and death and restoring the kingdom of God for Israel and the entire world!

Before ascending into heaven, Jesus gave His disciples one last mission: Tell the world the good news. The promised King has come, and eternal life is available to all through Him. Empowered by the Holy Spirit, the disciples set out on this mission, and it is one we, as the church, continue today.

Living counter-culturally, as members of the body of Christ, we commit ourselves to self-sacrificially love God and love others. We obey His commands as we corporately proclaim the gospel, both in word and deed. Through our words we invite people to experience eternal life through faith in Jesus. Through our actions we live out the implications of the gospel, helping to heal the brokenness caused by sin and build a world where *all of creation* thrives. Even amid the difficulties of life, we resist the false gods of this world to find our hope and comfort in the one true God because our ultimate allegiance is to His kingdom.

CHAPTER 5: RESTORATION

REVELATION

In the final pages of the story, we are told that one day our Savior and King, Jesus Christ, will return to fully restore the kingdom of God. God's plan of salvation will be complete. Sin, evil, death, and Satan will be no more. When this happens, believers will not escape to a far-off world; we will stay here. Heaven and earth will be reunited, and all of creation will be perfectly restored.

In a world with no sin, believers will perfectly love God and love others. We will live out our divine design as image bearers, reflecting the glory of God and thriving alongside all creation in the fullness of our restoration. We will live in the kingdom of God, under His rule, and love and worship Him forever.

As we study the Bible, it is easy for us to forget this larger story and focus on what a single passage means for us as individuals today. But every passage in the Bible is designed to point us to a larger message about who God is, who we are in Him, and what it means for us to live in His world. Through Christ, God has redeemed humanity so that we might live in shalom—peace and wholeness—with Him for eternity. By centering our understanding of Galatians within the larger storyline of the Bible, we are able to guard ourselves against misinterpreting Scripture. We are also able to keep the main thing the main thing, which is the glory of our triune God—the Father, the Son, and the Holy Spirit.

From Genesis to Revelation,
every word, event, and character
is interconnected and points
to an overarching message
about God's redemption of
humanity through Jesus Christ.

TIMELINE *of* PAUL'S MINISTRY

DATE	EVENT	SCRIPTURE
AD 33*	Paul's Conversion on the Road to Damascus	Acts 9:1-20
AD 33/34	Spends three years in Arabia	Gal. 1:17
AD 36/37	Meets with Peter in Jerusalem, flees to Tarsus	Acts 9:26-30; Gal. 1:18-21
AD 37–45	Lives and ministers in Syria/Cilicia	Gal. 1:21-24
AD 44–47	Ministry with Barnabas in Antioch	Acts 11:25-26
AD 46	Visits Jerusalem during the famine	Acts 11:27-30
AD 46–47	First Missionary Journey Writes Galatians	Acts 13:4–14:26
AD 48	Returns to Jerusalem for the Jerusalem Council	Acts 15
AD 49–52	Second Missionary Journey Writes 1&2 Thessalonians	Acts 15:36–18:22
AD 52–57	Third Missionary Journey Writes 1 & 2 Corinthians	Acts 18:23-21:17; 1 Cor. 16:1-8; 2 Cor. 2:1-4; 7:8-16
AD 57–62	Paul is arrested in Jerusalem, transferred to Caesarea, and imprisoned in Rome (house arrest) Writes Ephesians, Philippians, Colossians, and Philemon	Acts 21:27–28:31
AD 62–64	Released from house arrest and travels to Spain on his fourth missionary journey Writes 1 Timothy & Titus	Titus 3:12; 2 Tim. 4:13,20
AD 64	Arrested and imprisoned in Rome again Writes 2 Timothy	2 Tim. 2:9; 4:6
AD 64–67	Martyred	

*All dates are approximate and may vary by source.[1]

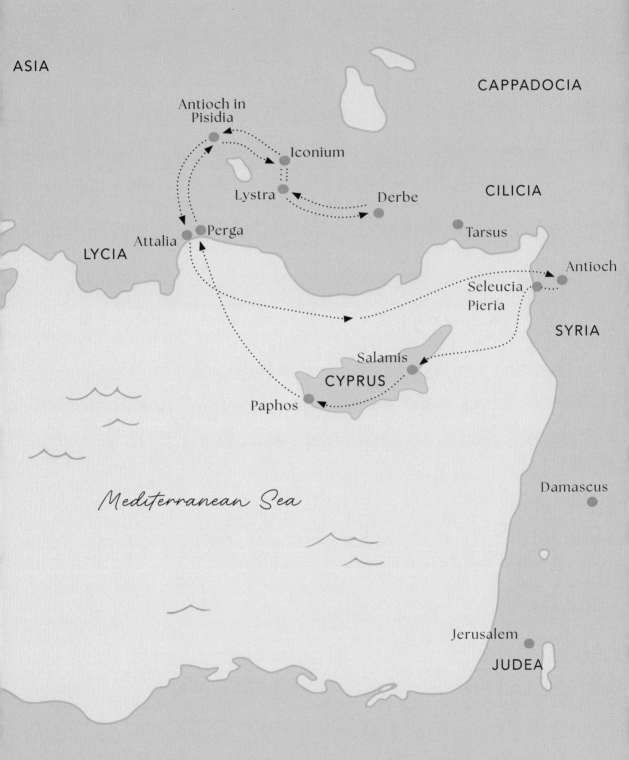

MAP of PAUL'S MINISTRY

GALATIA

ASIA

CAPPADOCIA

Antioch in Pisidia

Iconium

CILICIA

Lystra

Derbe

Tarsus

Antioch

Perga

Seleucia Pieria

Attalia

LYCIA

SYRIA

Salamis

CYPRUS

Paphos

Damascus

Mediterranean Sea

Jerusalem

JUDEA

WATCH

Watch the Session One video and take notes below.

Now, through this week's teaching video, let's zoom in on the story of Galatians together, focusing on its historical, cultural, and literary context.

1. What is *context* and why should studying it be an essential part of our Bible study process?

2. Who is the author of Galatians? | *Historical Context*

3. When was Galatians written? | *Historical Context*

4.   Who is the audience for Galatians? | *Cultural Context*

5.   Why was Galatians written? | *Cultural Context*

6.   What is the genre of Galatians, and what are its key themes and ideas? | *Literary Context*

Looking for more?

If you're leading a group, check out the leader guide found at lifeway.com/livefree.

Paul's Defense of
GOSPEL
FREEDOM

GALATIANS 1

Paul is writing to the churches in the region of Galatia. However, one thing hinders his letter from being well-received—his reputation. False teachers have been spreading lies about Paul, telling the Galatian believers that he is self-serving, dishonest, and devoid of authentic spiritual authority. So, in the first chapter of his letter to the Galatians, he will share about his testimony and early years of ministry to refute these falsehoods. He realizes that to convince the Galatians they are being led astray by a false gospel, he must first demonstrate that he is a trustworthy source and worth listening to. From Paul's example we're reminded that our spiritual reputation and testimony can either hinder or help advance the proclamation of the gospel.

Day One

READ GALATIANS

Read or listen to an audio version of the entire book of Galatians. Then answer the questions that follow.

What questions do you have after reading through Galatians?

What are your initial thoughts after reading through the book?

In one sentence, summarize your understanding of the main idea of Galatians.

Day Two

INTRODUCTION & GREETING (1:1-5)

Paul opens his letter to the Galatians with a greeting that establishes his authority and reminds them of the God who has graciously rescued them from their sins.

> ¹ Paul, an apostle—not from men or by man, but by Jesus Christ and God the Father who raised him from the dead— ² and all the brothers who are with me: To the churches of Galatia. ³ Grace to you and peace from God the Father and our Lord Jesus Christ, ⁴ who gave himself for our sins to rescue us from this present evil age, according to the will of our God and Father. ⁵ To him be the glory forever and ever. Amen.

GALATIANS 1:1-5

DIGGING DEEPER

An *apostle* is someone who has been directly taught and sent out on mission by Jesus Christ. These people have the authority to speak on behalf of Jesus and their writings are considered Scripture.[1]

1. In **1:1**, Paul introduces himself as an *apostle* and mentions two sources of apostolic authority. Which one is greater?

   Why do you think Paul begins the letter by making this distinction?

Throughout the study, we will compare verses in different Bible translations. Good online resources to compare Bible translations include biblehub.com and biblegateway.com. You can use the chart below to learn a little more about the different translations we will use in this study.[2]

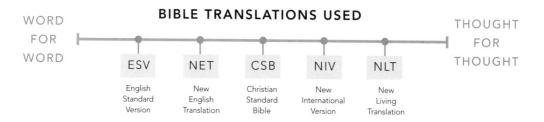

BIBLE TRANSLATIONS USED

WORD FOR WORD ————— ESV — NET — CSB — NIV — NLT ————— THOUGHT FOR THOUGHT

ESV	NET	CSB	NIV	NLT
English Standard Version	New English Translation	Christian Standard Bible	New International Version	New Living Translation

2. Look up **1:2** in the NIV and NLT. In addition to Paul, who is sending this message to the Galatians?

   Are you surprised by who is included in this group? Why or why not?

3. Fill in the table below to summarize how Paul describes the work of God the Father and Jesus Christ in **1:1-4**.

	GOD THE FATHER	JESUS CHRIST
1:1		
1:4		

4. Read Ephesians 2:1-5:

> [1] And you were dead in your trespasses and sins [2] in which you previously walked according to the ways of this world, according to the ruler of the power of the air, the spirit now working in the disobedient. [3] We too all previously lived among them in our fleshly desires, carrying out the inclinations of our flesh and thoughts, and we were by nature children under wrath as the others were also. [4] But God, who is rich in mercy, because of his great love that he had for us, [5] made us alive with Christ even though we were dead in trespasses. You are saved by grace!

How does this passage help you understand why Paul says we need to be rescued in **1:4**?

5. Reflect on Paul's description of God the Father and Jesus Christ. Why do you think he decides to end his greeting in **1:5** by ascribing glory to God?

6. **REFLECT & RESPOND:** Look back to Paul's description of God the Father and Jesus Christ in **1:1-4**. What are some practical ways you can glorify God for His gracious gift? Give one or two examples.

Day Three

ONE TRUE GOSPEL (1:6-10)

Paul wastes no time in sharing the reason for his letter. He is frustrated that the Galatians have walked away from the gospel truth he taught them. He wants to make sure they know what they are hearing from the Judaizers about the gospel is not true!

GALATIANS 1:6-10

DIGGING DEEPER

The Judaizers were a group of Jewish Christians who believed faith in Jesus *and* adherence to the Mosaic law were required for salvation and that these requirements applied to both the Jews and the Gentiles. (See p. 50 for more on the Judaizers and legalism.)

7. How does Paul describe the Galatians' actions in **1:6**?

The Galatians are turning away from:

_____

The Galatians are turning to:

8. What comparison does Paul make between the "different" gospels that the Galatians are being taught and the gospel of Jesus Christ in 1:6-7? Check the correct answer below.

    ☐ The different gospels help clarify the gospel of Christ.

    ☐ The different gospels are more confusing than the gospel of Christ.

    ☐ The different gospels are contrary to the gospel of Christ.

    For more, read "Let's Talk About: The Gospel" (p. 32).

9. **REFLECT & RESPOND:** In today's current culture, there is an overflow of information about Christianity available online. Through content avenues like sermons and social media posts, people can help others grow in their understanding of Christianity. However, what's said isn't always true and may lead people to internalize information that is contrary to the faith it claims to represent.

    What are some examples of "different gospels" that are being taught today, either from church pulpits or online?

    What is the danger of believing these modern-day false gospels?

    How can we be more discerning about the spiritual information we consume in these spaces?

10. Compare **1:7** in the CSB and the NIV. Fill in the chart below to indicate what words or phrases are used.

CSB	NIV
"_____ you"	"_____ you into _____"
"want to _____ the gospel of Christ"	"trying to _____ the gospel of Christ"

How does comparing **1:7** in these two translations help you understand the impact of these "different gospels"?

11. Who is the "we" Paul is referring to in **1:8-9**?

The Greek translation for "a curse" is *anathema*, which means condemned to hell.[3] Why do you think Paul believes this should be the end result of those who are preaching "different gospels" to the Galatians?

12. In **1:10**, Paul asks some questions to refute false information that was being spread about him. What was he being accused of? Is there any merit to these claims? Explain your answer, using Galatians 1:1-10 to help with your response.

13. <u>**REFLECT & RESPOND:**</u> As Christians, sometimes we have to fight against pleasing people. Whether it's motivated by fear or an unhealthy desire to be celebrated or affirmed, giving into this temptation leads us to choose the approval of man over the approval of Christ.

   Describe a situation in which you were tempted to please others rather than serve Christ. Did you give into temptation? Why or why not?

   Read Psalm 139:23-24. What insight do these verses provide into how we can overcome this temptation?

LET'S TALK ABOUT

The Gospel

Galatians 1:6-9

The word *gospel* is derived from the Greek word *euangelion*, which literally means "good news." This term was originally used to announce various types of news, ranging from victory in battle to the birth of a child.[4] In Scripture, *euangelion* takes on a spiritual meaning, as it is used to announce the good news that the promised Messiah, Jesus Christ, has come to earth. While many people associate the gospel with the first four books of the New Testament, which describe the life and ministry of Jesus, they aren't the first place in Scripture where the gospel is described.

We receive the first announcement about God's plan of salvation back in Genesis 3. (See "Zoom Out: The Story of the Bible" on pages 12-16.) God created the world and entrusted its care to His image bearers, Adam and Eve. However, they chose to

disobey God's instructions, leading to sin and destruction instead of the environment of *shalom* (peace) God had created.

Then in Genesis 3:15, as God punished Adam, Eve, and the serpent for rebelling, He told them, "I will put hostility between you and the woman, and between your offspring and her offspring. He will strike your head, and you will strike his heel." This verse is often referred to as the *protoeuangelion*, or the "first gospel." God promised that sin would not prevail forever and that, one day, one of Eve's descendants would emerge victorious over it!

The rest of the Old Testament builds off this promise, as we see God continue to make promises (or covenants) to redeem humanity. Therefore, when we come to

Matthew 1:1 and learn about Jesus's birth, it is good news because it is the fulfillment of all the promises God made throughout the Old Testament.

When sin entered the world, it sought to destroy everything. It created a counter pathway to the life God designed for us. As we read through the Old Testament, we observe the devastation produced when we choose sin's door to "life." But because Jesus the Son came to earth, died on the cross, and was resurrected, we are no longer bound by the power of sin. He set us free, and through Him we are able to experience life with God. This new life brings *shalom* for us individually and corporately. Then one day, when Christ returns, He will heal all of creation from the effects of sin, and we will live in *shalom* for eternity.

This is the gospel!

> We are no longer bound by the power of sin. Jesus set us free, and through Him we are able to experience life with God.

Day Four

PAUL'S TESTIMONY, PART 1 (1:11-16)

Paul knows the Judaizers have been telling the Galatians mistruths about him. Specifically, that he does not have any authority to teach the gospel. So, before he can show the Galatians why the Judaizers are misleading them, he first has to prove that he is worth listening to.

DIGGING DEEPER

For Paul, Judaism was a way of life based on the beliefs and practices of the Torah, but also on the historic traditions of the Jewish people. For his past self, this necessitated his participation in a movement to defend these traditions against Christians.[5]

---

[11] For I want you to know, brothers and sisters, that the gospel preached by me is not of human origin. [12] For I did not receive it from a human source and I was not taught it, but it came by a revelation of Jesus Christ. [13] For you have heard about my former way of life in Judaism: I intensely persecuted God's church and tried to destroy it. [14] I advanced in Judaism beyond many contemporaries among my people, because I was extremely zealous for the traditions of my ancestors. [15] But when God, who from my mother's womb set me apart and called me by his grace, was pleased [16] to reveal his Son in me, so that I could preach him among the Gentiles, I did not immediately consult with anyone.

GALATIANS 1:11-16

---

14. In **1:11-12**, Paul emphasizes the true source of the gospel he preaches. Fill in the chart below to summarize what he says.

Who Paul *did not* receive the gospel from	
Who Paul *did* receive the gospel from	

Why is he making this distinction for his readers? Look back to **1:10** for help with your answer.

15. Compare **1:13** in the CSB (on previous page), ESV, and NET. What word is used in place of "intensely" in the following two translations?

ESV _____

NET _____

What do these descriptions reveal about the way Paul was persecuting the church?

16. In **1:13-15**, Paul shares about his life before Christ. We are given more detail about his story in Acts 7:57–8:3 and Philippians 3:4-6. Read both of these passages and then note below what you learn. (Note: "Saul" was Paul's Jewish name.)

Before Christ, Paul was:

17. In **1:15-16**, Paul lists three things that God did on his behalf. Note them below.

a.

b.

c.

What was the goal of God's work in Paul's life?

18. Reflect on Paul's salvation story. How does what he shares in **1:16** help support his claim in **1:12-13**?

19. **REFLECT & RESPOND:** What tends to make us believe that our past actions can prevent God from using us for ministry?

In these moments, how can Paul's testimony encourage us?

Sadly, many Christians around the world are still being persecuted for their faith. Take a few moments to pray for these brothers and sisters, asking that God would protect, encourage, and provide for them. Visit christianresponse.org or persecution.com to learn more about the persecuted members of the global church and ways you can support them.

Day Five

PAUL'S TESTIMONY, PART 2 (1:17-24)

Paul continues to share his testimony to defend his apostolic authority. His after-conversion experience shows how he received his information about the gospel from one primary source, Jesus Christ.

> [17] I did not go up to Jerusalem to those who had become apostles before me; instead I went to Arabia and came back to Damascus. [18] Then after three years I did go up to Jerusalem to get to know Cephas, and I stayed with him fifteen days. [19] But I didn't see any of the other apostles except James, the Lord's brother. [20] I declare in the sight of God: I am not lying in what I write to you. [21] Afterward, I went to the regions of Syria and Cilicia. [22] I remained personally unknown to the Judean churches that are in Christ. [23] They simply kept hearing, "He who formerly persecuted us now preaches the faith he once tried to destroy." [24] And they glorified God because of me.

GALATIANS 1:17-24

20. Why is Paul intentional about telling us he didn't speak with the apostles in Jerusalem following his conversion (1:17)? Look back to 1:12 for help with your answer.

DIGGING DEEPER

The apostles who came before Paul were Peter, Andrew, James the son of Zebedee, John, Philip, Bartholomew, Thomas, Matthew, James the son of Alphaeus, Thaddaeus, Simon the Zealot, and Judas Iscariot. Matthias took Judas's place after he died (Matt. 10:2-4; Acts 1:23-26).

21. In **1:17-21**, Paul shares about where he goes after he encounters Christ on the road to Damascus. Use the map to illustrate his journey by labeling each city with a number that corresponds with its order in Paul's travels. (#1 = Damascus, #2 = Arabia, and so on.)

    Then write the letter "J" in the region where the Judean churches were located.

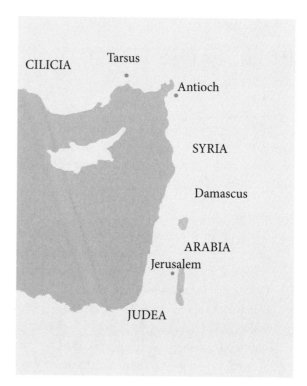

22. Look back to **1:18-19**. Fill in the chart below to summarize Paul's journey to Jerusalem.

After how many years did Paul go to Jerusalem?	
How long did he stay?	
Who did he see while he was there?	
Why might these people be considered influential by Paul's readers? Look up John 1:42 for help with your answer.	

23. How does the Judean church respond to reports about Paul's ministry (**1:22-24**)?

In light of Paul's life before Christ, why is their response significant?

24. **REFLECT & RESPOND:** After his conversion, Paul spends many years in solitude with God, learning gospel truth from Him. Why do we as believers need to spend time in silence and solitude with God?

What obstacles prevent us from regularly practicing this spiritual habit? Which do you struggle with most?

REFLECTION

UPWARD: What did God teach you about Himself through Galatians 1?

INWARD: How would your life change if you believed this truth?

OUTWARD: Share what you learned this week with a friend or family member.

CLOSE IN PRAYER

Thank God for being present with you in your study time and ask Him to help you live out the truth you learned this week in Galatians 1.

DISCUSS

Discuss the following questions with your Bible study group. A more extensive leader guide is available for free download at **lifeway.com/livefree**.

1.   (Question 4, p. 27) Read Ephesians 2:1-5. How does this passage help you understand why Paul says we need to be rescued (1:4)?

(Question 6, p. 27) **REFLECT & RESPOND:** Look back to Paul's description of God the Father and Jesus Christ in 1:1-4. What are some practical ways you can glorify God for His gracious gift? Give one or two examples.

2.   (Question 10, p. 30) How does comparing 1:7 in the CSB and NIV help you understand the impact of the "different gospels" the Galatian Christians encountered?

(Question 9, p. 29) **REFLECT & RESPOND:** What are some examples of "different gospels" that are being taught today, either from church pulpits or online? What is the danger of believing these modern-day false gospels? How can we be more discerning about the spiritual information we consume in these spaces?

3. (Question 17, p. 36) What was the goal of God's work in Paul's life?

    (Question 19, p. 36) **REFLECT & RESPOND:** What tends to make us believe that our past actions can prevent God from using us for ministry? In these moments, how can Paul's testimony encourage us?

4. (Question 23, p. 39) How does the Judean church respond to reports about Paul's ministry (1:22-24)? In light of Paul's life before Christ, why is their response significant?

    (Question 24, p. 39) **REFLECT & RESPOND:** After his conversion, Paul spends many years in solitude with God, learning gospel truth from Him. Why do we as believers need to spend time in silence and solitude with God? What obstacles prevent us from regularly practicing this spiritual habit? Which do you struggle with most?

5. (p. 40) **REFLECTION:**

    Upward: What did God teach you about Himself through Galatians 1?

    Inward: How would your life change if you believed this truth?

    Outward: How can you share what you learned this week with a friend or family member?

WATCH

Watch the Session Two video and take notes below.

TO ACCESS THE VIDEO SESSIONS, USE THE INSTRUCTIONS
IN THE BACK OF YOUR BIBLE STUDY BOOK.

43

Freedom from
THE LAW

GALATIANS 2

W e learn from Paul's letter that the Judaizers were telling the Galatians they had to live like the Jews in order to be Christians. These false teachers claimed to be leading the Galatians to the life with God they desired. But the additional regulations placed on them—most notably circumcision—created an extra burden and heavy weight Jesus never intended for them to bear. This week we will read about how Paul calls out this false doctrine twice, once to the apostles and then directly to Peter. With boldness and courage, Paul will declare how we are unable to earn our salvation. Freedom from sin comes only through faith.

Day One

READ GALATIANS

Read or listen to an audio version of the entire book of Galatians.
Use the space below to note any repeated words or phrases
you notice.

REPEATED WORDS/PHRASES

What do these repeated words indicate about important themes or
ideas that are present in Galatians?

Day Two

A MEETING IN JERUSALEM (2:1-5)

This week, Paul shares about a trip he took to Jerusalem to defend preaching the gospel to the Gentiles. In a bold act of courage, Paul meets with the apostles to ensure that the truth of salvation *by faith alone* remains intact as a foundational truth of Christianity.

> ¹ Then after fourteen years I went up again to Jerusalem with Barnabas, taking Titus along also. ² I went up according to a revelation and presented to them the gospel I preach among the Gentiles, but privately to those recognized as leaders. I wanted to be sure I was not running, and had not been running, in vain. ³ But not even Titus, who was with me, was compelled to be circumcised, even though he was a Greek. ⁴ This matter arose because some false brothers had infiltrated our ranks to spy on the freedom we have in Christ Jesus in order to enslave us. ⁵ But we did not give up and submit to these people for even a moment, so that the truth of the gospel would be preserved for you.
>
> ――――――――――
>
> GALATIANS 2:1-5

1. After his conversion, Paul spent many years serving in ministry in relative obscurity. How long was Paul doing ministry before his trip to Jerusalem (**2:1**)?

    Why was Paul's development in the background essential for his ability to be faithful as his public ministry to the Gentiles grew?

2. Which of the following best explains Paul's motivation for meeting with the religious leadership (**2:2**)? Check the correct answer.

☐ Paul wants to make sure they approve of what he is teaching the Gentiles.

☐ Paul wants to defend the gospel message he received from Christ, making sure everyone was preaching that salvation came through faith, not works of the law.

☐ Paul is questioning his call to ministry and needs them to affirm whether he should continue preaching.

During the time of the early church, the theological belief of justification by works was hotly contested. However, Paul was committed to arguing against it to help the Christian community hold to true doctrine. One such instance can be found in Act 15.[1]

3. Read Acts 15:1-21 and then number the events listed below in the order they appear.

__ James affirms Paul's message by recounting God's eternal plan to save all people, including the Gentiles. He then gives instructions as to what the Gentiles need to be taught about the essentials of Christian living.

__ Peter speaks to the apostles and elders, sharing how God destined for both Jews and Gentiles to be saved by faith.

__ Paul and his travel companions are met with opposition from Pharisees who said Gentile believers had to be circumcised and keep the Law of Moses.

__ Paul and Barnabas share with the Jewish leaders about their ministry with the Gentiles.

__ Paul and his travel companions travel to Jerusalem, sharing about their ministry to the Gentiles along the way.

4. What does the religious leadership not require Titus to do?

Considering Titus's background, why is this a significant victory (**2:3**)?

How does Paul describe those who disagreed with this decision (**2:4**)? Fill in the blanks from the CSB:

"*Some false brothers had* _____

our _____ *to* _____ *on the*

freedom we have in Christ Jesus in order to

_____ *us.*"

5. What reason does Paul give as to why he and Titus resisted the demands of the "false brothers" (**2:5**)?

6. **REFLECT & RESPOND:** While Paul is the author of this letter, he mentions several people he worked with to minister to the Gentiles and defend the gospel. Who are the people you would consider your "coworkers" in the faith? Pray for God to strengthen your relationships.

If you are in need of ministry coworkers, pray for God to give you wisdom for how you can meet other like-minded believers and the courage to take the first step of faith in response to what He tells you to do.

CIRCUMCISION

A religious rite performed as a sign of the covenant that God made with Abraham in Genesis 17. The *circumcision group* is the group of Jewish Christians who believed this religious practice alongside faith in Jesus was required for salvation, for both the Jews and the Gentiles.

For more, read "Let's Talk About: Legalism" (p. 50).

LET'S TALK ABOUT

Legalism

Galatians 2:4-5

Legalism is the belief that our salvation is directly linked to our actions, both the ones we perform and the ones we abstain from. It is a belief that is rooted in the covenant God made with Israel (Ex. 19–20). Before Christ, the Israelites sought right relationship with God through their obedience to the Mosaic law. But after Christ's death and resurrection, their relationship with the law changed.

Jewish Christians wrestled with the question of how they should view the law. Some, like Paul, saw the law as a guide designed to point us to godliness. Others, like the "false brothers" Paul mentions in Galatians 2:4, believed that adherence to the law was still required to attain God's favor and receive salvation. Historically, these "false brothers" were called Judaizers. They were Jewish Christians whose teachings of justification by works of the law promoted legalism.

During the time of Paul, the Judaizers taught that Jews and Gentiles could earn God's favor through faith in Jesus and by obeying the Mosaic law, which included circumcision for men. Much of what Paul wrote in Galatians is designed to refute this idea, showing how it is impossible for us to earn God's favor because it is impossible for us to perfectly follow God's law.

Even though most of us are not being told we need to obey Jewish religious customs to be saved, we still struggle with legalism. Often, legalistic teachings are disguised as teachings on how we can maintain our holy or sinless status before God. For example, they may classify wearing certain clothes or makeup, or listening to certain music as sinful actions that prevent one from receiving God's favor and eternal salvation. For some, legalism may show up as the belief that obedience earns God's blessing or love. Perhaps if we stop reading our Bibles or going to church for a season God will become angry with us and withhold His love and favor from us.

In the same way that adherence to the Mosaic law cannot save us, adherence to these artificial standards of holiness or perfection cannot save us either. The key problem with legalism is that it promotes the idea that we have the capacity on our own to meet God's standard for holiness. The sobering truth is, we don't. This is why we need Jesus. Only He was able to live a sinless life, pay the penalty for our sin, and overcome death. He did all of this out of the overflow of His love for us. So, all we have to do is receive His gift of salvation by faith in Jesus. We have been *justified*, or declared to be in right standing with God, because of Jesus!

Do we still need to obey God's commandments? Yes. But we don't obey in order to receive God's favor; we obey out of gratitude for having already received it through Jesus. No matter what we do, God's love for us will never change. We cannot earn His favor or His blessing. While our sinful actions can hinder our fellowship with God, once we place our faith in Jesus our salvation is secure, and we can't do anything to lose it (John 10:28-29). While legalism claims to be a pathway to salvation, in reality it leads people to spiritual bondage. Only by our faith in Christ are we able to *live free*.

> We don't obey in order to receive God's favor; we obey out of gratitude for having already received it through Jesus.

Day Three

AFFIRMED BY THE APOSTLES (2:6-10)

The apostles formally recognize the authenticity of Paul's ministry to the Gentiles during his meeting with them in Jerusalem. This is a significant moment for Paul because it affirms both his apostolic authority and the gospel message he is preaching.

> [6] Now from those recognized as important (what they once were makes no difference to me; God does not show favoritism)—they added nothing to me. [7] On the contrary, they saw that I had been entrusted with the gospel for the uncircumcised, just as Peter was for the circumcised, [8] since the one at work in Peter for an apostleship to the circumcised was also at work in me for the Gentiles. [9] When James, Cephas, and John—those recognized as pillars—acknowledged the grace that had been given to me, they gave the right hand of fellowship to me and Barnabas, agreeing that we should go to the Gentiles and they to the circumcised. [10] They asked only that we would remember the poor, which I had made every effort to do.

GALATIANS 2:6-10

7. Compare **2:6** in the CSB and the NLT, and then answer the questions below.

   Who is Paul referring to when he says "those recognized as important"?

   ☐   Government officials

   ☐   The apostles—James, Peter, and John

   ☐   The "false brothers"

   What is Paul's perspective of this group of people? Explain why.

8. Look up the word *entrusted* in a dictionary or thesaurus and write a definition for it that best fits the way it is used in **2:7**.

ENTRUSTED

Based on your definition, describe the weight of responsibility that accompanies Paul's ministry assignment.

9. In **2:8**, Paul shares about how his ministry is compared to the ministry of Cephas. What group of people have each of these men been sent out to serve? Check the correct answers below.

PETER	☐ The Jews/Circumcised
	☐ The Gentiles/Uncircumcised
PAUL	☐ The Jews/Circumcised
	☐ The Gentiles/Uncircumcised

DIGGING DEEPER

Jesus gave His disciple Simon the name *Cephas*, which in Aramaic means "rock" (John 1:42). The Greek translation of "rock" is Peter.

10. **REFLECT & RESPOND:** In the same way that Paul was entrusted with sharing the gospel with the Gentiles, you and I are entrusted with a specific ministry by God. Read 2 Corinthians 5:17-21. What ministry have we been entrusted with?

What are some ways we can be more intentional about stewarding this responsibility well? Give one or two examples.

11. Who do the apostles recognize has been at work in the lives of Peter and Paul? How does this affirmation support Paul's claim in **1:11-12**?

    How do James, Cephas, and John indicate their acceptance of Paul (**2:9**)?

12. In **2:10**, what are Paul and Barnabas asked to remember? Why do you think this task is emphasized? Read James 1:27 and Matthew 25:34-40 to help with your answer.

13. **REFLECT & RESPOND:** Peter and Paul had unique ministry assignments that were connected to their upbringing and life experiences. Take a few moments to consider your own upbringing and life experiences. How do you think these have uniquely equipped you to minister to others?

Day Four

CONFRONTING PETER (2:11-14)

Paul shares another story that illustrates his efforts to defend the gospel against false teaching. Paul witnesses Peter mistrust the Gentiles, and confronts him about his misplaced theological beliefs. For a church community that struggled with issues of division, this story would especially illustrate the power of right doctrine, showing how what we believe impacts how we view God and treat those around us.

> [11] But when Cephas came to Antioch, I opposed him to his face because he stood condemned. [12] For he regularly ate with the Gentiles before certain men came from James. However, when they came, he withdrew and separated himself, because he feared those from the circumcision party. [13] Then the rest of the Jews joined his hypocrisy, so that even Barnabas was led astray by their hypocrisy. [14] But when I saw that they were deviating from the truth of the gospel, I told Cephas in front of everyone, "If you, who are a Jew, live like a Gentile and not like a Jew, how can you compel Gentiles to live like Jews?"
>
> ──────────
>
> GALATIANS 2:11-14

14. Fill in the blanks below to describe how Paul engages with Peter (**2:11**).

    "I _____ him to his _____, because he stood

    _____."

15. What situation did Paul witness that led him to approach Peter in this manner (**2:12-13**)?

16. This is not the first time Peter had been criticized about who he was eating with. Read Acts 11:2-9 to learn about a previous encounter he had with the circumcision group and then answer the following question.

Why does Paul use the word "hypocrisy" to describe Peter's actions (**2:13**)?

17. How did Peter's actions impact the believers who were with him (**2:13**)?

18. **REFLECT & RESPOND:** Peter was a significant figure in the early church. He was one of the original disciples, and in Matthew 16:18, Jesus tells him how he will be an instrumental part of building the church. After denying Jesus before His crucifixion, Jesus reinstated Peter into ministry, commissioning him to spiritually feed the church. People would have deeply respected Peter as church leader and teacher and been easily influenced by his actions.

As ministers of reconciliation (2 Cor. 5), why do we need to remember the power we have to influence people? What can happen if we forget?

19. Describe how Peter's actions "deviate[d] from the truth of the gospel" (2:14).

20. **REFLECT & RESPOND:** Paul rebuked Peter because he was not living in light of the truth of the gospel. Peter had been accepted by God by grace. However, his separation from Gentile Christians showed his unwillingness to treat them with the same grace he had received from God.

Why is it difficult for us to offer others the same grace we have received from God?

What truth from Scripture can we internalize to help us resist the temptation to withhold grace from other people? Look up Ephesians 2:8-9 for help with your answer.

Day Five

JUSTIFIED BY FAITH (2:15-21)

Paul explains the error of Peter's behavior, showing how his actions pointed to the false belief that justification came by obeying the law rather than by faith. This theological truth is Paul's main point for his letter to the Galatians, and in future chapters we will see him go to lengths to defend it.

> [15] We are Jews by birth and not "Gentile sinners," [16] and yet because we know that a person is not justified by the works of the law but by faith in Jesus Christ, even we ourselves have believed in Christ Jesus. This was so that we might be justified by faith in Christ and not by the works of the law, because by the works of the law no human being will be justified. [17] But if we ourselves are also found to be "sinners" while seeking to be justified by Christ, is Christ then a promoter of sin? Absolutely not! [18] If I rebuild those things that I tore down, I show myself to be a lawbreaker. [19] For through the law I died to the law, so that I might live for God. [20] I have been crucified with Christ, and I no longer live, but Christ lives in me. The life I now live in the body, I live by faith in the Son of God, who loved me and gave himself for me. [21] I do not set aside the grace of God, for if righteousness comes through the law, then Christ died for nothing.

GALATIANS 2:15-21

21. In **2:15-16**, Paul reminds Peter of the gospel truth they had learned from Christ, specifically how we are justified and cleansed of our sin. Fill in the blanks below to summarize what he says:

What DOESN'T justify us _____

What DOES justify us _____

22. Read Hebrews 11:1. How does this verse help clarify your understanding of what it means to live by faith?

JUSTIFICATION
The act by which God declares us righteous and thereby not guilty for our sins because of our faith in Christ who paid for our sin on the cross (Rom. 3:21-26).

23. If we don't earn God's favor by obeying His commands, what is our motivation for obeying Him (**2:17-20**)?

WORKS OF THE LAW

Actions done to live in adherence to the Mosaic law that was given to Israel in Exodus 20–40 and Leviticus 1–7; 23. These laws governed how Israel lived in community with one another and their ceremonies of worship. Consisting of more than six hundred laws, this set of instructions was designed to help Israel love God and love one another.[2]

24. What is the value of Christ's death if we are able to become righteous through obedience to God's commandments (**2:21**)?

25. **REFLECT & RESPOND:** Even though we have been saved by grace, some of us still struggle with trying to earn God's favor. What are some actions we perform or abstain from because we believe they make us more acceptable to God?

What is the downside to embracing these legalistic behaviors?

Why is it important for us to remember that God blesses us with salvation because of His love for us, not our good works?

REFLECTION

UPWARD: What did God teach you about Himself through Galatians 2?

INWARD: How would your life change if you believed this truth?

OUTWARD: Share what you learned this week with a friend or family member.

CLOSE IN PRAYER

Thank God for being present with you in your study time and ask Him to help you live out the truth you learned this week in Galatians 2.

I have been crucified with Christ, and I no longer live, but Christ lives in me. The life I now live in the body, I live by faith in the Son of God, who loved me and gave himself for me.

Galatians 2:20

DISCUSS

Discuss the following questions with your Bible study group. A more extensive leader guide is available for free download at **lifeway.com/livefree**.

1. (Question 5, p. 49) What reason does Paul give as to why he and Titus resisted the demands of the "false brothers" (2:5)?

   (Question 6, p. 49) **REFLECT & RESPOND:** Who are the people you would consider your "coworkers" in the faith? Pray for God to strengthen your relationships. If you are in need of ministry coworkers, pray for God to give you wisdom for how you can meet other like-minded believers and the courage to take the first step of faith in response to what He tells you to do.

2. (Question 8, p. 53) Share the definition you came up with for *entrusted* (2:7). Based on your definition, describe the weight of responsibility that accompanies Paul's ministry assignment.

   (Question 10, pp. 53-54) **REFLECT & RESPOND:** Read 2 Corinthians 5:17-21. What ministry have we been entrusted with? What are some ways we can be more intentional about stewarding this responsibility well? Give one or two examples.

3.   (Question 19, p. 57) Describe how Peter's actions "deviate[d] from the truth of the gospel" (2:14).

(Question 20, p. 57) **REFLECT & RESPOND:** Why is it difficult for us to offer others the same grace we have received from God? What truth from Scripture can we internalize to help us resist the temptation to withhold grace from other people? Look up Ephesians 2:8-9 for help with your answer.

4.   (Question 23, p. 59) If we don't earn God's favor by obeying His commands, what is our motivation for obeying Him (2:17-20)?

(Question 25, p. 60) **REFLECT & RESPOND:** What are some actions we perform or abstain from because we believe they make us more acceptable to God? What is the downside to embracing these legalistic behaviors? Why is it important for us to remember that God blesses us with salvation because of His love for us, not our good works?

5.   (p. 61) **REFLECTION:**

Upward: What did God teach you about Himself through Galatians 2?

Inward: How would your life change if you believed this truth?

Outward: How can you share what you learned this week with a friend or family member?

WATCH

Watch the Session Three video and take notes below.

TO ACCESS THE VIDEO SESSIONS, USE THE INSTRUCTIONS
IN THE BACK OF YOUR BIBLE STUDY BOOK.

65

Freedom by FAITH

GALATIANS 3:1–14

Starting this week, we will watch as Paul methodically unfolds his argument against justification by the law. Paul will utilize his deep knowledge of the Jewish faith to craft a powerful argument, showing why justification by the law is not only wrong, but a misinterpretation of the Scriptures the Jews hold dear. By appealing to their experience with the Holy Spirit, Abraham, and the Mosaic law, Paul clearly demonstrates why our sin makes it impossible for us to earn God's favor. Before we celebrate the good news of salvation through Christ, we must remember our utter inability to overcome the power and penalty of sin. Only then can we see the true cost of legalism and the freedom that comes by faith.

READ GALATIANS

Read or listen to an audio version of the entire book of Galatians. Match each of the verses below to the Old Testament verse it references.

Galatians 3:6	Deuteronomy 27:26
Galatians 3:8	Genesis 21:10
Galatians 3:10	Genesis 12:7
Galatians 3:11	Leviticus 18:5
Galatians 3:12	Genesis 15:6
Galatians 3:13	Isaiah 54:1
Galatians 3:16	Genesis 22:18
Galatians 4:27	Deuteronomy 21:23
Galatians 4:30	Habakkuk 2:4

What do the amount of Old Testament quotations in Galatians indicate about the importance of knowing God's whole story—the Old Testament and the New Testament?

Day Two

THE HOLY SPIRIT'S POWER (3:1-6)

In this chapter, Paul begins to defend the doctrinal beliefs he presented in 2:15-21. He will use the Galatians' experience with the Holy Spirit as the first of three different examples to prove why justification only comes by faith.

[1] You foolish Galatians! Who has cast a spell on you, before whose eyes Jesus Christ was publicly portrayed as crucified? [2] I only want to learn this from you: Did you receive the Spirit by the works of the law or by believing what you heard? [3] Are you so foolish? After beginning by the Spirit, are you now finishing by the flesh? [4] Did you experience so much for nothing—if in fact it was for nothing? [5] So then, does God give you the Spirit and work miracles among you by your doing the works of the law? Or is it by believing what you heard— [6] just like Abraham who believed God, and it was credited to him for righteousness?

GALATIANS 3:1-6

1. Which of the following best describes Paul's sentiment in **3:1**?

   □   Paul is frustrated that the Galatians have forgotten their first-hand experience of seeing Jesus crucified.

   □   Paul is frustrated that the Galatians have forgotten about the powerful message he preached to them about Christ's crucifixion.

2. In **3:2-5**, Paul uses the Galatians' experience with the Holy Spirit to show how foolish their actions were. He does this by asking a series of questions that lead them to choose between two options. For the chart on the next page, fill in the blanks from the CSB (included above) to summarize each option.

PAUL'S QUESTION	OPTION 1	OPTION 2
a. How did they receive the Spirit (3:2)?	"by the _____ of the _____"	"by _____ what you _____"
b. Who initiated their salvation process (3:3a)?	"After_____ by the _____"	
c. How are they trying to grow spiritually (3:3b)?		"are you now _____ by the _____?"
d. How does God give them the Spirit and work miracles in their lives (3:5)?	"by your _____ the _____ of the law"	"by _____ what you _____"

3. Compare the information in the two columns above. Note the differences below.

DIFFERENCES

_____

4. **REFLECT & RESPOND:** The Holy Spirit's work in our lives serves as a testimony to the authenticity of our conversion. Take a few moments to reflect on your spiritual growth journey. In what ways has the Holy Spirit transformed your life? Give one or two examples.

For more, read "Let's Talk About: Abraham & Faith" (p. 72).

5. What did Abraham do as a result of his faith in God (**3:6**)? Look up Hebrews 11:8 for help with your answer.

6. Read Romans 4:3-5. What is the difference between righteousness being credited to Abraham and Abraham earning righteousness?

RIGHTEOUSNESS

Being in right moral standing with God because of one's faith in Christ.

7. **REFLECT & RESPOND:** Abraham's belief in God was made evident through his obedience to God's commands. (For example, see Gen. 22:1-19.) Think about a current life situation in which you need to be like Abraham and believe God. What is one practical step you can take this week to walk in obedience to God's direction?

LET'S TALK ABOUT

Abraham & Faith

Galatians 3:6-14

Paul frequently mentions Abraham in Galatians because Abraham was highly revered by the Jews. In Genesis, God made a covenant with Abraham, promising to bless him and bless the world through him (Gen. 12; 15; 17). This blessing of salvation was to be passed down to Abraham's offspring or descendants. During the time of Paul, the Jews believed their identity as physical descendants of Abraham was their "salvation insurance." Paul uses this belief to challenge the Judaizers' ideas about justification by works. By highlighting Abraham as their model for righteousness, Paul shows that if Abraham was saved by faith, then the same must be true of those who receive his promised blessing.

The author of Hebrews defines faith as "the reality of what is hoped for, the proof of what is not seen" (Heb. 11:1). Faith is the process of believing something to be true, even though we don't have all the physical evidence that it is true. In the words of Dr. Tony Evans, "Faith is acting like God is telling the truth."[1] If God says it, we can believe it because He never lies, changes His mind, or fails to make good on a promise. His faithfulness is the anchor and foundation of our faith.

Our faith in Jesus is an affirmation that salvation is only available through Him. In believing this, we relinquish control over our own lives and submit fully to His authority over all things. By our faith we are then justified, declared righteous by God. He graciously frees us from the consequences of our sins and to experience the fruit of His presence, which is abundant life.

However, our faith is more than an intellectual exercise. It is made evident through our actions, specifically our obedience. When we believe God, we walk in obedience to His commands. Abraham models this for us, as his faith in God led him to obey God's call to leave his homeland and follow Him (Gen. 12:4). Likewise, our faith should lead us to live in obedience to the way of Jesus.

As you read through Galatians, remember that the fruit of our faith is not only about what we have been saved from; it's also about what we have been saved to experience. Faith leads to life because faith ultimately enables us to live out our divine design as image bearers. By faith we live to reflect God's character to those around us and to help all of creation flourish and thrive (Gen. 1:26-28). By faith we get to live free as we experience *shalom* with God for eternity.

> Faith leads to life because faith ultimately enables us to live out our divine design as image bearers.

ABRAHAM'S FAITH (3:7-9)

Paul focuses on the life of Abraham, a historical figure the Jews highly revered, as his second example in proving justification by faith alone. The Jews believed that their salvation was linked to their ethnicity. Since they were the physical descendants of Abraham, they believed they would inherit the promises God had made to Abraham and his descendants. However, Paul will show them that God's promise of blessing is not based on a physical lineage, but a spiritual one.

> [7] You know, then, that those who have faith, these are Abraham's sons. [8] Now the Scripture saw in advance that God would justify the Gentiles by faith and proclaimed the gospel ahead of time to Abraham, saying, All the nations will be blessed through you. [9] Consequently, those who have faith are blessed with Abraham, who had faith.
>
> ───────
>
> GALATIANS 3:7-9

ABRAHAM'S SONS

The heirs and recipients of the promise of blessing God made to Abraham in Genesis 12; 15; and 17. All those who believe in Christ by faith are heirs of God's promise and thereby sons of Abraham.

8. Are women who have placed their faith in Christ considered to be "Abraham's sons" (**3:7**)? Circle the correct answer.

Yes   No

9. Look back to Genesis 12:3. Who did God have in mind when He spoke these words to Abraham (**3:8**)?

What does this teach us about God's plan to redeem the Gentiles (non-Jews)?

10. Historically, the Jews believed only the physical descendants of Abraham would receive God's promised blessing. How do you think they reacted after hearing Paul say God's promised blessing had always included both the Jews and Gentiles?

11. **REFLECT & RESPOND:** Scholars believe that the first announcement of God's plan to save humanity in Scripture is recorded in Genesis 3:15. Right before He banishes Adam and Eve from the garden of Eden, God promises that one day the evil that has produced sin will be conquered by the "seed of the woman." As we read through Scripture, we learn that this "seed" is God the Son, Jesus Christ.

For more, refer back to "Let's Talk About: The Gospel" (p. 32).

What does this truth communicate about God's character?

What does this truth communicate about His love for us?

12. In Genesis 15, Abraham has a vision about the blessing God promised him in Genesis 12. Read Genesis 15:1-6 and then answer the questions below.

What problem does Abraham express to God (Gen. 15:2)?	
How does Abraham intend to fix it (Gen. 15:3)?	
How does God respond to Abraham's plan (Gen. 15:4-5)?	
How does Abraham respond to God's promise (Gen. 15:6)?	

13. What do we need to do to receive the blessing God promised to Abraham (**3:9**)?

14. **REFLECT & RESPOND:** Abraham waited twenty-five years for God to provide him with a son. However, years later God asked Abraham to sacrifice his son as a burnt offering. Read Genesis 22:11-19 to learn more and then answer the following questions.

What do you learn about faith from Abraham's actions and God's response?

How does this story help you understand what it means to live by faith?

Day Four

THE CURSE OF THE LAW (3:10-12)

Today we come to the third stop on our journey through Paul's defense of the gospel. Similarly to his discussions about the Holy Spirit and Abraham, Paul will continue to defend the gospel message by explaining the purpose of the Mosaic law. The law has one very important purpose, but it is much different than what the Judaizers think it is.

> [10] For all who rely on the works of the law are under a curse, because it is written, Everyone who does not do everything written in the book of the law is cursed. [11] Now it is clear that no one is justified before God by the law, because the righteous will live by faith. [12] But the law is not based on faith; instead, the one who does these things will live by them.
>
> ───────
>
> GALATIANS 3:10-12

DIGGING DEEPER

"[There are] only two ways in which it is possible to approach God. Either we approach God completely without merit of our own, on the ground of his grace alone, or we approach him on the grounds of our own merits."[2]
– R. Alan Cole

15. Is it possible to do everything written in the law? Why or why not (**3:10**)?

16. What happens to us if we don't obey God's law perfectly? Read Romans 3:23 and Romans 6:23 to help with your answer.

17. **REFLECT & RESPOND:** In Romans 7:14-21, Paul talks about the struggle he experiences in his pursuit of godliness. Even though he tries to live in obedience to God's commands, he doesn't always do the right thing. Have you ever had this same experience? Share about it below.

How do our struggles with sin help confirm Paul's words in **3:10**?

18. Read **3:11-12** in the NLT and then answer the questions below.

	The way of f_____	The way of l_____
What two "ways" does Paul mention in these verses?		
For each "way," what does a person have to do to have life?		
Which way is a dead end and which way actually leads to life?		

19. What type of "life" is Paul referring to in **3:11-12**? Check the
    correct answer.

    _____ a. Eternal life with God because our sins have been forgiven.

    _____ b. Abundant life with God because our fellowship with Him
             has been restored.

    _____ c. Both a and b

20. **REFLECT & RESPOND:** Why is it important for us to talk about
    sin and the consequences for not following God's law before we talk
    about the good news of Christ rescuing us?

    What do we miss out on if we don't do this?

Day Five

CHRIST AND OUR CURSE (3:13-14)

Yesterday, Paul reminded the Galatians (and us) of a sobering truth: Our disobedience of God's holy and perfect law comes with the harsh curse of death. Today we get the good news that because of His love and grace Christ took on this curse for us!

> [13] Christ redeemed us from the curse of the law by becoming a curse for us, because it is written, Cursed is everyone who is hung on a tree. [14] The purpose was that the blessing of Abraham would come to the Gentiles by Christ Jesus, so that we could receive the promised Spirit through faith.
>
> ———————
>
> GALATIANS 3:13-14

21. Why did Christ need to redeem us? Why were we unable to redeem ourselves (**3:13**)?

22. Read 1 Peter 2:24. How did Christ redeem us from the curse of the law (**3:13**)?

23. Jesus Christ is sovereign and omnipotent, which means He could have chosen any way to die for our sins. Based on Paul's words in **3:13**, what is the significance of Jesus dying on a cross made of wood from a tree?

24. What did Christ's sacrifice accomplish for the Gentiles (**3:14**)?

25. In **3:14**, who is Paul referring to when he says "we"? Circle the correct answer. Look up Romans 4:16 for help with your answer.

The Jews   The Gentiles   Jews and Gentiles

26. Fill in the table below to summarize the three examples Paul uses in **3:1-14** as he builds his argument to defend against justification by works. Look back at the daily summaries for help with your answer.

Example 1 (3:1-6)	
Example 2 (3:7-9)	
Example 3 (3:10-14)	

27. **REFLECT & RESPOND:** What sins did Jesus Christ pay for on your behalf? List a few below, and then write a prayer of gratitude, thanking Him for His gracious sacrifice.

REFLECTION

UPWARD: What did God teach you about Himself through Galatians 3:1-14?

INWARD: How would your life change if you believed this truth?

OUTWARD: Share what you learned this week with a friend or family member.

CLOSE IN PRAYER

Thank God for being present with you in your study time and ask Him to help you live out the truth you learned this week in Galatians 3:1-14.

DISCUSS

Discuss the following questions with your Bible study group. A more extensive leader guide is available for free download at **lifeway.com/livefree**.

1. (Question 6, p. 71) Read Romans 4:3-5. What is the difference between righteousness being credited to Abraham and Abraham earning righteousness?

   (Question 7, p. 71) **REFLECT & RESPOND:** Think about a current life situation in which you need to be like Abraham and believe God. What is one practical step you can take this week to walk in obedience to God's direction?

2. (Question 13, p. 76) What do we need to do to receive the blessing God promised to Abraham (3:9)?

   (Question 14, p. 77) **REFLECT & RESPOND:** What do you learn about faith from Abraham's actions and God's response in Genesis 22:11-19? How does this story help you understand what it means to live by faith?

3. (Question 18, p. 79) Read 3:11-12 in the NLT and then discuss the chart on page 79.

(Question 20, p. 80) **REFLECT & RESPOND:** Why is it important for us to talk about sin and the consequences for not following God's law before we talk about the good news of Christ rescuing us? What do we miss out on if we don't do this?

4. (Question 24, p. 82) What did Christ's sacrifice accomplish for the Gentiles (3:14)?

(Question 27, p. 83) **REFLECT & RESPOND:** Spend time in prayer together, thanking Jesus for His gracious sacrifice on your behalf.

5. (p. 84) **REFLECTION:**

Upward: What did God teach you about Himself through Galatians 3:1-14?

Inward: How would your life change if you believed this truth?

Outward: How can you share what you learned this week with a friend or family member?

WATCH

Watch the Session Four video and take notes below.

TO ACCESS THE VIDEO SESSIONS, USE THE INSTRUCTIONS
IN THE BACK OF YOUR BIBLE STUDY BOOK.

87

Free Through

CHRIST

GALATIANS 3:15–4:7

Paul knows his Scripture! In Galatians 3:1-14, he quoted six Old Testament passages to prove how the blessings made to Abraham apply to his "offspring" by faith. Historically, the Jews thought this offspring only included them, but Paul shows how God always intended to save everyone who believes in Him through faith. Paul's argument is clear, but it leaves us with one major question: *If the law can't save us, then why did God give it to us?* In the portion of Galatians we'll study this week, Paul addresses this question head on. He will use one more example in his argument against justification by faith, and will show how the law did not replace God's promise to Abraham but was intentionally given by God to lead us to Christ. God knew we wouldn't be able to fight sin on our own, and out of the overflow of His love for us, He made sure we wouldn't have to.

Day One

READ GALATIANS

Read or listen to an audio version of the entire book of Galatians. Use the space below to note the words/phrases Paul uses to identify who we are under the law and who we are in Christ.

UNDER THE LAW WE ARE	IN CHRIST WE ARE

Day Two

THE PLAN DIDN'T CHANGE (3:15-18)

After the covenant God made with Abraham by faith, some people may have believed that God had replaced faith with performance of the law as the requirement for receiving His blessing. However, Paul explains that God did not change His mind, because God never goes back on His word.

> [15] Brothers and sisters, I'm using a human illustration. No one sets aside or makes additions to a validated human will. [16] Now the promises were spoken to Abraham and to his seed. He does not say "and to seeds," as though referring to many, but referring to one, and to your seed, who is Christ. [17] My point is this: The law, which came 430 years later, does not invalidate a covenant previously established by God and thus cancel the promise. [18] For if the inheritance is based on the law, it is no longer based on the promise; but God has graciously given it to Abraham through the promise.

GALATIANS 3:15-18

1. Compare **3:15** in the CSB, NIV, and NLT.

   CSB (above): No one sets aside or makes additions to a _____ _____.

   NIV: Just as no one can set aside or add to a _____ _____, so it is in this case.

   NLT: Just as no one can set aside or amend an _____ _____, so it is in this case.

   Using these varying translations, write your own paraphrase of Galatians 3:15.

God made Abraham promises in several passages in Genesis (e.g. Gen. 12:1-7; 13:15; 15:4-20; 17:8; 24:7). In each of these passages, God promises blessing to Abraham and his offspring. The Hebrew word used for offspring is *sperma* ("seed"), and it can be used in the plural and the singular (Gal. 3:16).[1]

Why is it not possible to add anything to this type of agreement?

2. Which of the following was the intended recipient of God's promise (**3:16**)?

    ☐   Abraham and Israel, his physical offspring

    ☐   Christ

    ☐   Everyone who believes in Christ by faith

    ☐   All of the above

3. If the law came 430 years after the promise to Abraham, why does it not "invalidate" those promises God previously made? Look back to **3:15** for help with your answer.

For more, read "Let's Talk About: The Law" (p. 94).

4. Why isn't the basis for Abraham receiving the inheritance both the law *and* the promise (**3:18**)? Read Ephesians 2:8-9 for help with your answer.

5. **REFLECT & RESPOND:** What are some things people try to add to the gospel today? Give one or two examples.

6. **REFLECT & RESPOND:** In Genesis 15, God performed a special ceremony to confirm the covenantal promises He made to Abraham. During this ceremony, God demonstrated how the promises He made to Abraham in Genesis were unconditional. Abraham did not have to meet a specific standard to receive the promise. God was going to keep His word because He is always faithful (2 Tim. 2:13).

   What are some ways you have seen God be faithful in your life? Share one or two examples.

   How does a regular remembrance of God's faithfulness help us trust Him more?

LET'S TALK ABOUT

The Law

Galatians 3:17

In Galatians, whenever Paul uses the term "the law," he is referring to the Mosaic law found in the Old Testament. This law consisted of more than six hundred commandments that God gave to Israel, preserved for us in the book of Exodus. After rescuing Israel from Egypt, God entered into a covenant with them in the wilderness. This agreement, known as the Mosaic Covenant, bound both parties to uphold their end of the bargain. Obedience to the covenant would bring about great blessings, and disobedience to the covenant resulted in consequences or curses (see Deut. 28). However, since God is perfectly faithful, Israel would be the only party to suffer the consequences of breaking the covenant.

The Mosaic law is divided into three main categories: the civil law, the ceremonial law, and the moral law. The civil laws provided a system of order to Israel's life as a nation by giving time- and culture-specific instructions on how Israel should coexist together. These laws can be found in Exodus 21–23 and cover topics such as murder, compensation for your donkey falling into someone else's pit, and returning your neighbor's cloak at night if you take it as collateral. While these verses describe regulations that might seem strange and irrelevant to us now, they were given to govern Israel's life during a specific period of time. Therefore, although they were necessary for them, they do not apply to us.

The ceremonial laws were a set of commandments that governed how Israel worshiped God. These laws included statutes that detailed the sacrifices Israel had to make in order to cleanse themselves from their sins. Other worship statutes were given to help Israel remember God's work in their lives.

There was a specific set of feasts and festivals they observed every year to commemorate their deliverance out of slavery and the forty years spent in the wilderness. Lastly, these laws helped to set Israel apart as God's people. Practices such as circumcision and Passover would fall into this category. Similar to the civil law, because of Christ, Scripture does not call us as believers to observe the ceremonial law.

The moral laws are a reflection of God's character. These laws include the Ten Commandments and establish boundaries for how people should relate to God and to each other. Unlike the civil and ceremonial laws, the moral laws are still applicable to believers today. While we are not required to follow them for our salvation, they provide a blueprint for how we can live like Christ. When we follow the moral laws, we are fulfilling our divine purpose to reflect God's character to the world, loving Him with our heart, soul, and mind, and loving our neighbors as ourselves.

As we've seen in Galatians 3, the Mosaic law was designed to show Israel how to have right standing before God, living as His people in His world. However, as Paul teaches, the law was never intended to save us. Instead, it exposes the ways in which we fall short of God's holy standards. This is evident throughout the Old Testament, as Israel struggles to follow the law. Even when they offer sacrifices for their sins, the cleansing is only temporary, as they will inevitably sin again. The law serves only to highlight our need for a savior. Paul shows us that this savior is not our good works, but Jesus Christ.[2]

> When we follow the moral laws, we are fulfilling our divine purpose to reflect God's character to the world, loving Him with our heart, soul, and mind, and loving our neighbors as ourselves.

THE LAW LEADS US TO FAITH (3:19-22)

Yesterday we studied how Paul explained that God didn't change His plan. The law was never intended to be the new way to receive God's blessings. Today we will see Paul demonstrate how the law works in partnership with faith, serving as a mirror to reflect our sin and our need for God's grace.

DIGGING DEEPER

In 3:20, "the underlying assumption . . . is that an arrangement between a person and God that has mediators is inferior to an arrangement that has no mediators, because the latter arrangement is directly from God. Paul is also assuming that the arrangement with Abraham, the covenant established through Genesis 12 and 15, is one that had no mediation; for that reason alone it is superior."[3]

–Scot McKnight

> 19 Why, then, was the law given? It was added for the sake of transgressions until the Seed to whom the promise was made would come. The law was put into effect through angels by means of a mediator. 20 Now a mediator is not just for one person alone, but God is one. 21 Is the law therefore contrary to God's promises? Absolutely not! For if the law had been granted with the ability to give life, then righteousness would certainly be on the basis of the law. 22 But the Scripture imprisoned everything under sin's power, so that the promise might be given on the basis of faith in Jesus Christ to those who believe.
>
> GALATIANS 3:19-22

7. Read **3:19-20** in the NLT and then answer the questions below.

Why did God give Israel the law?	
How long was the law designed to last?	
Through whom did God give Israel the law?	

8. Look up the word *contrary* in a thesaurus and write a few of its antonyms (opposites) below (**3:21**).

    CONTRARY

9. Considering the words you wrote above, which option best characterizes the relationship between the law and the promise?

    ☐ The law is unrelated to the promise.

    ☐ The law does the same thing as the promise.

    ☐ The law leads people to the promise.

10. In **3:22**, Paul shares how the law acts like a mirror that shows us a reflection of ourselves that, on our own, we can't get away from or change. What specifically does the law show us about ourselves? Read Romans 3:9-20 for help with your answer.

11. **REFLECT & RESPOND:** Why is it necessary for us to regularly reflect on our own life and confess any sin that we have committed? Look up 1 John 1:9 for help with your answer.

What might prevent us from doing this?

How does unconfessed sin impact your relationship with God? How does it impact your relationship with others?

12. **REFLECT & RESPOND:** In God's plan of redemption, He not only promised to save us, He ensured that all of us would be able to clearly see our sin and our inability to save ourselves. How does the remembrance of this truth change the way we interact with others?

What is one step you can take to better embody this humility with your friends/family this week?

Day Four

FREED BY CHRIST (3:23-28)

We are unable to keep God's law perfectly because of our sinful nature. Every time we try, we will inevitably fail. This is why our good works could never help us receive God's blessing of salvation. Instead, the law highlights our desperate need for a savior who will free us from the bondage of sin. Today, Paul will show us that Christ Jesus is that Savior, and how, when He came, we were set free!

> [23] Before this faith came, we were confined under the law, imprisoned until the coming faith was revealed. [24] The law, then, was our guardian until Christ, so that we could be justified by faith. [25] But since that faith has come, we are no longer under a guardian, [26] for through faith you are all sons of God in Christ Jesus. [27] For those of you who were baptized into Christ have been clothed with Christ. [28] There is no Jew or Greek, slave or free, male and female; since you are all one in Christ Jesus.
>
> ———————
>
> GALATIANS 3:23-28

13. Read **3:23** in the CSB (above). What two words does Paul use to describe our relationship to the law before Jesus Christ came into the world? Circle them in the printed text above, and write them in the spaces below.

    C_____

    I_____

    Based upon your understanding of these two words, draw a picture that illustrates our relationship to the law.

14. In **3:24-26**, Paul talks about how before Christ the law was our "guardian." He uses a similar word at the beginning of 1 Corinthians 4:15. Write the word below.

GALATIANS 3:24	1 CORINTHIANS 4:15

GUARDIAN

The Greek word translated *guardian* here denotes non-family members of the household, typically slaves, who were put in charge of a child. They were often tutors and disciplinarians who supervised the child until they reached the age of maturity or inheritance.[4]

15. What did the law teach us? Look back to **3:19** for help with your answer.

How did these "lessons" lead us to faith?

16. What changes occur when we are baptized in Christ (**3:27**)? Read the verses below and note what you learn.

Romans 6:4-14

Ephesians 4:22-24

17. In **3:28**, Paul mentions three different groups. List them below.

What relational dynamic within these groups has dissolved? Explain why.

18. **REFLECT & RESPOND:** Read **3:28** again. How do you think this truth would have impacted the Jewish Christians who believed the Gentiles needed to become like them to be saved?

How do you think this truth would have impacted the Gentile Christians who were being told that they had to assimilate to the practices of another ethnicity in order to be saved?

19. **REFLECT & RESPOND:** Paul closes this section by highlighting the unity and oneness that should characterize the church. How is this characteristic true of the church, both local and global?

How can we do better with living out our identity as one unified body?

What steps do you need to take to pursue oneness in your church community?

FREED TO BE SONS (3:29–4:7)

This week, we have been slowly going through the third example in Paul's defense of justification by faith. He has demonstrated to us how God's plan of redemption used the law to reveal our need for a Savior. On our own, we are unable to overcome the power of sin; we need help from someone greater than us, and that person is Christ! Today, Paul concludes this section of his letter by revealing the extent of what Christ's redemption has achieved for us.

> [29] And if you belong to Christ, then you are Abraham's seed, heirs according to the promise. [4:1] Now I say that as long as the heir is a child, he differs in no way from a slave, though he is the owner of everything. [2] Instead, he is under guardians and trustees until the time set by his father. [3] In the same way we also, when we were children, were in slavery under the elements of the world. [4] When the time came to completion, God sent his Son, born of a woman, born under the law, [5] to redeem those under the law, so that we might receive adoption as sons. [6] And because you are sons, God sent the Spirit of his Son into our hearts, crying, "Abba, Father!" [7] So you are no longer a slave but a son, and if a son, then God has made you an heir.
>
> GALATIANS 3:29–4:7

20. Read **3:29**. What word does Paul use to describe those of us who belong to Christ?

    _____ according to the promise

    Write a definition for that word below. Use a dictionary for help with your answer.

21. In **4:1-3**, Paul uses an analogy from the Roman legal system to describe the freedom we have in Christ. Fill in the chart below to summarize what he says.

Who is the heir under (4:2)?	
Who were we subject to when we were "children" (4:3)?	

22. When did God send Christ into the world (**4:4**)?

23. What does this teach us about the intentionality of God's plan of redemption?

> **REDEMPTION**
> The act of buying back or rescuing something or someone that was lost, enslaved, or in a state of bondage.

24. Fill in the blanks below to describe how we were transformed by Jesus's redemption (**4:5-7**).

Because of Jesus we went from being

s_____ to sin

to s_____ of God.

25. **REFLECT & RESPOND:** Look up Mark 14:32-38. What does Jesus's use of the phrase "Abba, Father" in this passage communicate about His relationship with God the Father?

Paul says the Holy Spirit who dwells in us calls out to God the Father with this same phrase (**4:6**). What does this communicate about the closeness of our relationship with God?

Is this how you view your relationship with God? Explain why or why not.

REFLECTION

UPWARD: What did God teach you about Himself through Galatians 3:15–4:7?

INWARD: How would your life change if you believed this truth?

OUTWARD: Share what you learned this week with a friend or family member.

CLOSE IN PRAYER

Thank God for being present with you in your study time and ask Him to help you live out the truth you learned this week in Galatians 3:15–4:7.

When the time came to completion, God sent his Son, born of a woman, born under the law, to redeem those under the law, so that we might receive adoption as sons.

Galatians 4:4-5

DISCUSS

Discuss the following questions with your Bible study group. A more extensive leader guide is available for free download at **lifeway.com/livefree**.

1. (Question 4, p. 92) Why isn't the basis for Abraham receiving the inheritance both the law and the promise (3:18)? Read Ephesians 2:8-9 for help with your answer.

    (Question 6, p. 93) **REFLECT & RESPOND:** What are some ways you have seen God be faithful in your life? Share one or two examples. How does a regular remembrance of God's faithfulness help us trust Him more?

2. (Question 10, p. 97) In 3:22, Paul shares how the law acts like a mirror that shows us a reflection of ourselves that, on our own, we can't get away from or change. What specifically does the law show us about ourselves? Read Romans 3:9-20 for help with your answer.

    (Question 11, pp. 97-98) **REFLECT & RESPOND:** Why is it necessary for us to regularly reflect on our own life and confess any sin that we have committed? Look up 1 John 1:9 for help with your answer. What might prevent us from doing this? How does unconfessed sin impact your relationship with God? How does it impact your relationship with others?

3. (Question 17, pp. 100-101) In 3:28, Paul mentions three different groups. What are they? What relational dynamic within these groups has dissolved? Explain why.

(Question 19, p. 101) **REFLECT & RESPOND:** Paul closes this section by highlighting the unity and oneness that should characterize the church. How is this characteristic true of the church, both local and global? How can we do better with living out our identity as one unified body? What steps do you need to take to pursue oneness in your church community?

4.   (Questions 22 & 23, p. 103) When did God send Christ into the world (4:4)? What does this teach us about the intentionality of God's plan of redemption?

(Question 25, p. 104) **REFLECT & RESPOND:** Look up Mark 14:32-38. What does Jesus's use of the phrase "Abba, Father" in this passage communicate about His relationship with God the Father? Paul says the Holy Spirit who dwells in us calls out to God the Father with this same phrase (4:6). What does this communicate about the closeness of our relationship with God? Is this how you view your relationship with God? Explain why or why not.

5.   (p. 105) **REFLECTION:**

Upward: What did God teach you about Himself through Galatians 3:15–4:7?

Inward: How would your life change if you believed this truth?

Outward: How can you share what you learned this week with a friend or family member?

WATCH

Watch the Session Five video and take notes below.

TO ACCESS THE VIDEO SESSIONS, USE THE INSTRUCTIONS
IN THE BACK OF YOUR BIBLE STUDY BOOK.

109

Children of the
FREE WOMAN

GALATIANS 4:8–31

Prior to writing this letter, Paul had invested a considerable amount of time ministering to the Galatians, nurturing their spiritual growth. So—like any good shepherd—Paul is concerned for his sheep. In this section, we will see him pause his defense of the gospel to express his heart for the Galatians. With love, he will honestly share how they are regressing in their faith and being deceived by individuals whose motives are not good. Then, he restarts his defense one final time. Using the story of Abraham, Sarah, and Hagar, he provides a powerful finale to this section of his letter, demonstrating why our hope for salvation is not in our efforts but in the grace of God.

Day One

READ GALATIANS

Read or listen to an audio version of the entire book of Galatians.
Choose one verse to memorize for the rest of the study. Practice
memorizing it by writing it out below three times.

1.

2.

3.

Day Two

TAKING A STEP BACK (4:8-11)

Taking a break from his defense of justification by faith, Paul expresses his concern that the Galatians' belief in a false gospel represents a regression in their faith.

> [8] But in the past, since you didn't know God, you were enslaved to things that by nature are not gods. [9] But now, since you know God, or rather have become known by God, how can you turn back again to the weak and worthless elements? Do you want to be enslaved to them all over again? [10] You are observing special days, months, seasons, and years. [11] I am fearful for you, that perhaps my labor for you has been wasted.
>
> GALATIANS 4:8-11

1. In **4:8-9**, Paul provides three characteristics of the things the Galatians were enslaved to before they became Christians. List them below.

    a.

    b.

    c.

    How do these characteristics measure up against the character of God?

2. Which is a more serious offense—worshiping idols when you don't know the truth or choosing to return to your idols after knowing the truth about God? Explain your answer.

3. **REFLECT & RESPOND:** Look up Colossians 2:8 and 2:20. What "weak and worthless elements" have you been influenced by or tempted to follow?

4. The "special days, months, seasons, and years" that Paul mentions in **4:10** refers to a set of feasts and festivals the Jews observed in accordance with the law. Read 2 Chronicles 8:13 and list below the feasts this verse mentions.

   Why were the Galatians observing these special festivals and feasts?

5. Look back over Galatians 1–2. What are some ways Paul has labored for the Galatians (**4:11**)?

6. **REFLECT & RESPOND:** Even though the Galatians had experienced the power of God at work in their lives, they were reverting back to their old ways of worshiping gods with no power. To worship an idol is to use a person, place, or thing as our ultimate source of comfort, identity, or security in place of God. What are some modern-day idols we worship?

Why are we tempted to go back to our idols after having experienced the power of God in our lives?

FALSE MOTIVES (4:12-20)

Paul offers a passionate plea, expressing his concern that those who are leading the Galatians away from the gospel have self-serving motives.

> ¹² I beg you, brothers and sisters: Become as I am, for I also have become as you are. You have not wronged me; ¹³ you know that previously I preached the gospel to you because of a weakness of the flesh. ¹⁴ You did not despise or reject me though my physical condition was a trial for you. On the contrary, you received me as an angel of God, as Christ Jesus himself.
>
> ¹⁵ Where, then, is your blessing? For I testify to you that, if possible, you would have torn out your eyes and given them to me. ¹⁶ So then, have I become your enemy because I told you the truth? ¹⁷ They court you eagerly, but not for good. They want to exclude you from me, so that you would pursue them. ¹⁸ But it is always good to be pursued in a good manner—and not just when I am with you. ¹⁹ My children, I am again suffering labor pains for you until Christ is formed in you. ²⁰ I would like to be with you right now and change my tone of voice, because I don't know what to do about you.

GALATIANS 4:12-20

7. How has Paul become like the Galatians? What about his actions is he hoping they imitate (**4:12**)? Read 1 Corinthians 9:19-23 for help with your answer.

8. How did the Galatians receive Paul the first time they met him (**4:13-14**)? How has their affection for him changed (**4:15-16**)? Note your responses in the following chart.

HOW THE GALATIANS TREATED PAUL THE FIRST TIME THEY MET HIM	HOW THE GALATIANS ARE CURRENTLY TREATING PAUL

9. What is the motivation of those who are preaching against Paul (**4:17-18**)?

10. In **4:19**, Paul uses a metaphor that helps explain the depth of his relationship with the Galatians. Fill in the blank below to help describe the significance of his words in this verse.

If Paul considers the Galatians his "children," then he is their m_____.

11. Think about the pain level of labor pains. What does Paul's use of this phrase communicate about his concern for the Galatians (**4:19**)?

What is driving his concern? Read Ephesians 4:11-15 for help with your answer.

12. **REFLECT & RESPOND:** As believers, we are called to make disciples, which requires us to spiritually invest in someone else's life. What does it look like for us to help someone grow into spiritual maturity?

How can we as disciple makers stay committed when, like Paul, we see those we are discipling straying away from the faith?

Day Four

HAGAR & SARAH (4:21-27)

Today and tomorrow, we will delve into the most complex passages in the book of Galatians. To illustrate the power of living by faith, Paul refers to the story of Abraham. Instead of waiting on God to fulfill His promise, Abraham and his wife Sarah take matters into their own hands. Although their solution created chaos, God remained faithful.

> [21] Tell me, you who want to be under the law, don't you hear the law? [22] For it is written that Abraham had two sons, one by a slave and the other by a free woman. [23] But the one by the slave was born as a result of the flesh, while the one by the free woman was born through promise. [24] These things are being taken figuratively, for the women represent two covenants. One is from Mount Sinai and bears children into slavery—this is Hagar. [25] Now Hagar represents Mount Sinai in Arabia and corresponds to the present Jerusalem, for she is in slavery with her children. [26] But the Jerusalem above is free, and she is our mother. [27] For it is written,
>
> Rejoice, childless woman,
> unable to give birth.
> Burst into song and shout,
> you who are not in labor,
> for the children of the desolate woman will be many,
> more numerous than those
> of the woman who has a husband.
>
> ———
> GALATIANS 4:21-27

DIGGING DEEPER

From Genesis 12–16, Abraham and Sarah were called Abram and Sarai. In Genesis 17, God gave them their new names (Abraham and Sarah) signifying the new reality of the covenant He had made with them.[1]

13. In order to understand the illustration Paul makes in **4:21-31**, take a few minutes to read Genesis 16:1-15 and Genesis 21:1-3. Then answer the questions below.

What problem is Sarah trying to solve?

For more, see "Let's Talk About: Sarah and Hagar" (p. 123).

According to Sarah, who is responsible for her problem?

What is Sarah's proposed solution?

How does Sarah's plan impact Sarah, Hagar, and Abraham?

What does God do in Genesis 21:1?

14. Let's go back to Paul's words in Galatians **4:21-27**. Fill in the chart below to summarize the details given about Hagar and Sarah and to help you follow Paul's illustration.

	SARAH	HAGAR
Who is the slave woman and who is the free woman (4:22)?		
Was her son born as a result of the flesh or through promise (4:23)?		
Which covenant does each woman represent: the Old Covenant (Mount Sinai) or the New Covenant (4:24)?		
What spiritual home does each woman represent: earthly (present) Jerusalem or heavenly Jerusalem (4:26)?		
What method of justification does each woman represent: works of the law or faith in the work of Christ?		

15. **REFLECT & RESPOND:** One of the reasons Paul uses the story of Sarah and Hagar is to illustrate the difference between living by faith and living by the flesh. Instead of waiting on God to fulfill His promise, Sarah and Abraham decided to fix their problem on their own. Have you ever chosen to fix a situation in your life instead of waiting on God to fix it? Describe that experience below.

What do we miss out on when we don't wait on God? How can we encourage ourselves to keep waiting, even when it's hard?

LET'S TALK ABOUT

Sarah and Hagar

Galatians 4:21-31

As we read through Galatians 4:21-31, it is important for us to focus on the goal of Paul's words. The story of Sarah and Hagar can produce mixed emotions for many of us—especially as we consider Sarah's infertility, or Hagar's life as an enslaved person and the lack of choice she had in sleeping with Abraham. However, Paul isn't addressing those issues in this section of Galatians. He isn't making a statement about Sarah's character or condoning Hagar's mistreatment. Instead, he is using their story figuratively to illustrate a more significant principle about living by faith and living by the flesh.

In his allegory, Paul quotes Isaiah 54:1, in which the prophet Isaiah predicts the deliverance of Israel from exile. Having spent such a long time experiencing the consequences of their sin, the Israelites felt weak and barren, doubting God's promises to Abraham. They feared they were not strong enough to have offspring as numerous as the stars in the sky (Gen. 15:5) and reoccupy the land of promise. Through Isaiah, God reminded Israel that just as Sarah became the mother of a whole nation, so Israel would again be filled with people. But, this restoration would extend *beyond* their return to Babylon and include *all* the spiritual descendants of Abraham.[2]

Even though she was barren, God was calling the nation of Israel to rejoice because the promise would be fulfilled. However, it wouldn't be because of their efforts but because of God's grace and the work of Christ.

Similarly, Paul is using the story of Sarah and Hagar to emphasize how God is fulfilling His promise to Abraham. Sarah, the mother whom God blessed, was not favored because of her efforts but solely because of God's grace. Therefore, those who live by faith are the spiritual children of Sarah.

Day Five

CHILDREN OF PROMISE (4:28-31)

Paul finishes his defense of the gospel message by reminding us of the opposition believers face from those who stand against the gospel. He encourages us to stand boldly as we hold onto the hope of our inheritance in Christ.

> [28] Now you too, brothers and sisters, like Isaac, are children of promise. [29] But just as then the child born as a result of the flesh persecuted the one born as a result of the Spirit, so also now. [30] But what does the Scripture say? "Drive out the slave and her son, for the son of the slave will never be a coheir with the son of the free woman." [31] Therefore, brothers and sisters, we are not children of a slave but of the free woman.
>
> GALATIANS 4:28-31

16. Who is Paul referring to when he says "brothers and sisters" (**4:28**)? Check the correct answer.

    ☐ The Jews

    ☐ The Gentiles

    ☐ Jews and Gentiles

17. How has the "child born as a result of the flesh" persecuted the "one born as a result of the Spirit" (**4:29**)? Read the passages below and note what you learn.

Genesis 21:8-10	
Acts 14:19	

18. In **4:30**, Paul quotes the words of Sarah from Genesis 21:10. For him, the "slave and her son" represents the Judaizers. Why does Paul encourage such a strong response toward them?

19. What are the eternal implications of the Galatians, and us, being children of the free woman (**4:31**)?

20. **REFLECT & RESPOND:** The way for us to become "children of the free woman" is made possible through the grace of God. How should we respond to the grace we've received?

    What is one thing you can do to reflect this truth in your walk with Christ?

REFLECTION

UPWARD: What did God teach you about Himself through Galatians 4:8-31?

INWARD: How would your life change if you believed this truth?

OUTWARD: Share what you learned this week with a friend or family member.

CLOSE IN PRAYER

Thank God for being present with you in your study time and ask Him to help you live out the truth you learned this week in Galatians 4:8-31.

DISCUSS

Discuss the following questions with your Bible study group. A more extensive leader guide is available for free download at **lifeway.com/livefree**.

1. (Question 2, p. 114) Which is a more serious offense—worshiping idols when you don't know the truth or choosing to return to your idols after knowing the truth about God? Explain your answer.

    (Question 6, p. 115) **REFLECT & RESPOND:** What are some modern-day idols we worship? Why are we tempted to go back to our idols after having experienced the power of God in our lives?

2. (Question 11, p. 118) Think about the pain level of labor pains. What does Paul's use of this phrase communicate about his concern for the Galatians (4:19)? What is driving his concern? Read Ephesians 4:11-15 for help with your answer.

    (Question 12, p. 118) **REFLECT & RESPOND:** As believers, we are called to make disciples, which requires us to spiritually invest in someone else's life. What does it look like for us to help someone grow into spiritual maturity? How can we as disciple makers stay committed when, like Paul, we see those we are discipling straying away from the faith?

3. (Question 14, p. 121) Take a few minutes to share how you filled in the chart on page 121 to summarize the details given about Hagar and Sarah.

    (Question 15, p. 122) **REFLECT & RESPOND:** Have you ever chosen to fix a situation in your life instead of waiting on God to fix it? What do we miss out on when we don't wait on God? How can we encourage ourselves to keep waiting, even when it's hard?

4. (Question 19, p. 125) What are the eternal implications of the Galatians, and us, being children of the free woman (4:31)?

    (Question 20, p. 125) **REFLECT & RESPOND:** How should we respond to the grace we've received? What is one thing you can do to reflect this truth in your walk with Christ?

5. (p. 126) **REFLECTION:**

    Upward: What did God teach you about Himself through Galatians 4:8-31?

    Inward: How would your life change if you believed this truth?

    Outward: How can you share what you learned this week with a friend or family member?

WATCH

Watch the Session Six video and take notes below.

TO ACCESS THE VIDEO SESSIONS, USE THE INSTRUCTIONS
IN THE BACK OF YOUR BIBLE STUDY BOOK.

129

Spirit-led
FREEDOM

GALATIANS 5

Up to this point, Paul's letter to the Galatians has mainly focused on establishing his authority and defending why justification can only come through faith. Having laid that theological foundation, he goes on to explain how we can experience the freedom that comes from living by God's grace, not our merit. For Paul, freedom is not about living a life without any boundaries but living a life that is ordered by the boundaries of godliness. The more we deny our flesh and say yes to the things of God (all by the power of the Holy Spirit), the more we are able to experience life as it was designed to be lived. God created us to be image bearers, living for His glory and for the good of others. When we live like this, we are free from the burden of sin and are free to experience an abundant life—full of love and joy.

Day One

READ GALATIANS

Read or listen to an audio version of the entire book of Galatians.
Write any fresh observations or questions below.

Continue memorizing the verse you chose last week. Write the verse
on a few notecards and place them in locations you will see them often
(e.g. your bathroom mirror, car dashboard, or refrigerator door).

Day Two

STAND FIRM (5:1-6)

Trying to earn God's favor doesn't bring us freedom but takes it away. We can only experience true freedom when we embrace grace and live by faith.

> [1] For freedom, Christ set us free. Stand firm, then, and don't submit again to a yoke of slavery. [2] Take note! I, Paul, am telling you that if you get yourselves circumcised, Christ will not benefit you at all. [3] Again I testify to every man who gets himself circumcised that he is obligated to do the entire law. [4] You who are trying to be justified by the law are alienated from Christ; you have fallen from grace. [5] For we eagerly await through the Spirit, by faith, the hope of righteousness. [6] For in Christ Jesus neither circumcision nor uncircumcision accomplishes anything; what matters is faith working through love.

GALATIANS 5:1-6

1. How does Paul tell us to respond to the freedom Christ has given us (**5:1**)?

   "_____ _____, then,

   and don't _____ again to a yoke of slavery."

2. Read **5:2-4**. What three consequences does Paul mention for those who decide to follow the Judaizers and get circumcised?

   a.

   b.

   c.

3. Why does a pursuit of justification by the law alienate us from the grace of Christ? Look up Galatians **5:4** in the NLT for help with your answer.

4. Look up the verses below and note what they teach us about why we can eagerly wait for "the hope of righteousness" (**5:5**).

    2 CORINTHIANS 1:22

    EPHESIANS 1:14

5. How is our faith in Christ displayed in our lives (**5:6**)?

6. **REFLECT & RESPOND:** Paul ends today's passage by mentioning how faith working through love matters more than any religious actions we might practice to gain God's favor. In what way do we as Christians elevate our religious practices over love for others? Give a few examples.

Day Three

FREE TO LOVE (5:7-15)

While enticing, false teaching is dangerous, and left unchecked it will negatively affect the freedom we have in Christ. But when we walk in truth, we will use our freedom to love others well, helping them flourish and live like Christ.

> [7] You were running well. Who prevented you from obeying the truth? [8] This persuasion does not come from the one who calls you. [9] A little leaven leavens the whole batch of dough. [10] I myself am persuaded in the Lord you will not accept any other view. But whoever it is that is confusing you will pay the penalty. [11] Now brothers and sisters, if I still preach circumcision, why am I still persecuted? In that case the offense of the cross has been abolished. [12] I wish those who are disturbing you might also let themselves be mutilated!
> [13] For you were called to be free, brothers and sisters; only don't use this freedom as an opportunity for the flesh, but serve one another through love. [14] For the whole law is fulfilled in one statement: Love your neighbor as yourself. [15] But if you bite and devour one another, watch out, or you will be consumed by one another.
>
> _____
>
> GALATIANS 5:7-15

7. In **5:7-9**, Paul uses two metaphors to describe how the Judaizers' false teaching has impacted the Galatians. Answer the question below to describe the meaning of his metaphors.

	METAPHOR #1 (5:7) RUNNING = THE CHRISTIAN LIFE	METAPHOR #2 (5:9) LEAVEN = FALSE TEACHING
How has the Judaizer's false teaching impacted the Galatians?		

8. In **5:10**, what two things is Paul confident about?

   a.

   b.

9. Read Galatians **5:11** in the NLT. What accusation is being spread about Paul? Why is it not true?

   What does Paul hope will happen to those who are spreading falsehoods about him? Why (**5:12**)?

10. Check the answer below that best describes the type of freedom Paul is referring to in **5:13**.

    ☐ Freedom to be and do whatever we desire

    ☐ Freedom to be and do whatever pleases God

    What is the ultimate goal of our freedom? What happens if we lose sight of this goal (**5:14-15**)?

11. Who else in the New Testament uses the same statement that Paul does in **5:14**?

Search the statement in an online Bible (such as biblegateway.com), and write the verse reference below.

12. **REFLECT & RESPOND:** How does the world's definition of freedom differ from the freedom we have in Christ?

For more, read "Let's Talk About: Freedom and Holiness" (p. 138).

When faced with the temptation to prioritize your personal desires over what glorifies God, how can you resist?

LET'S TALK ABOUT

Freedom and Holiness

Galatians 5:16-26

When Paul tells us how to use our freedom in Christ, he directs us to walk by the Spirit (5:16). This means surrendering ourselves to the Holy Spirit's work of sanctification in our lives. As we yield to God's commands and live in obedience, the Holy Spirit gradually transforms us to become more and more like Christ. He also brings us closer to God's goal for our lives—holiness.

All of us are born with a sinful nature, which leads us to choose our own way over God's way. Sin has corrupted many things since the time of Adam and Eve, including our ability to live out our divine design. God created humans to be image bearers, which means that we were designed to serve as His "image," reflecting His character to the world.

We were set apart as holy to show the world what God is like. Unfortunately, our sinful nature prevents us from doing this. However, through the power of the Holy Spirit, God is on a mission to restore what sin has corrupted.

Once we put our trust in Jesus Christ, the Holy Spirit initiates a gradual process of sanctification within us. The aim of this transformation is not merely to change our behavior, but to make us into a new person. It impacts the entirety of our being and leads to wholeness. As J. I. Packer put it, "personal holiness is personal wholeness—the ongoing reintegration of our disintegrated and disordered personhood as we pursue our goal of single-minded Jesus-likeness."[1]

People are desperately searching for wholeness and freedom, seeking to discover their authentic selves. To achieve this, they tend to relentlessly pursue happiness through indulgence in created things. But the Scripture shows us how true humanity can only be found in Christ, for genuine humanness is genuine Christlikeness. Living like Jesus did is what makes us genuinely human. We are called to imitate the character of Christ so that the things that hold us back from living whole and holy are left behind.[2]

When Paul calls us to walk in the Spirit, he is inviting us to be freed from sin and freed to live the only way we were created to live—as image bearers of our Triune God.

As we yield to God's commands and live in obedience, the Holy Spirit gradually transforms us to become more and more like Christ. He also brings us closer to God's goal for our lives—holiness.

DENYING THE FLESH (5:16-21)

True freedom leads us to Christlikeness. However, this process of spiritual transformation requires us to follow the Holy Spirit as we deny the desires of our flesh.

> [16] I say, then, walk by the Spirit and you will certainly not carry out the desire of the flesh. [17] For the flesh desires what is against the Spirit, and the Spirit desires what is against the flesh; these are opposed to each other, so that you don't do what you want. [18] But if you are led by the Spirit, you are not under the law.
> [19] Now the works of the flesh are obvious: sexual immorality, moral impurity, promiscuity, [20] idolatry, sorcery, hatreds, strife, jealousy, outbursts of anger, selfish ambitions, dissensions, factions, [21] envy, drunkenness, carousing, and anything similar. I am warning you about these things—as I warned you before—that those who practice such things will not inherit the kingdom of God.
>
> ———————
>
> GALATIANS 5:16-21

13. What do we have to surrender to "walk by the Spirit" (**5:16**)?
    Read Ephesians 5:18 for help with your answer.

14. Why is there a battle between the Spirit and our flesh (**5:17-18**)?

15. **REFLECT & RESPOND:** What biblical encouragement can we hold onto when we experience this battle in our lives? Look up 1 Corinthians 10:13 and Philippians 2:13 and note what you learn.

16. In **5:19-21**, Paul lists several acts of the flesh. Write them below, placing them in the category that best defines the attitude or action. Highlight the ones that are actions and place a star next to the ones that are attitudes.

SEXUALITY	RELIGION	RELATIONSHIPS	DRINKING

17. Which of the following best describes the group of people that Paul believes will not inherit the kingdom of God?

☐ Those who practice the works of the flesh at least once

☐ Those who habitually practice the works of the flesh without repentance

☐ Those who think about practicing the works of the flesh

18. **REFLECT & RESPOND:** Look back to **5:19-21**. Which of these attitudes or actions do you struggle with? Explain why.

Philippians 1:6 and 2:13 remind us that God is committed to living out the calling He has on our lives, which includes walking by the Spirit. Take a few moments to ask God for forgiveness for the actions/ attitudes you listed above. Then ask Him to help you resist your flesh and live a life controlled by the Holy Spirit.

Day Five

BEARING FRUIT (5:22-26)

As we deny our flesh, the Holy Spirit produces within us fruit—attributes of Christlikeness that reflect the holy character of God.

> ²² But the fruit of the Spirit is love, joy, peace, patience, kindness, goodness, faithfulness, ²³ gentleness, and self-control. The law is not against such things. ²⁴ Now those who belong to Christ Jesus have crucified the flesh with its passions and desires. ²⁵ If we live by the Spirit, let us also keep in step with the Spirit. ²⁶ Let us not become conceited, provoking one another, envying one another.
>
> ——————
>
> GALATIANS 5:22-26

19. What word does Paul use to describe actions of the flesh in **5:19**?

    (**5:19**) w_____ of the flesh

    (**5:22**) f_____ of the Spirit

20. Why didn't Paul say *works of the Spirit* in **5:22**? What distinction is he trying to make?

21. Why do you think Paul says "fruit" of the Spirit and not "fruits" of the Spirit (**5:22**)?

22. List each aspect of the fruit of the Spirit in the chart below along with a word that describes its opposite (**5:22-23**).

FRUIT OF THE SPIRIT	OPPOSITE
Love	Hate

23. What advice does Paul give at the end of chapter 5 (**5:24-26**)? Compare it to **5:15** and **3:28** and note what you learn below.

24. **REFLECT & RESPOND:** How do you see the fruit of the Spirit growing in your life? What does it look like for you to "keep in step with the Spirit"?

REFLECTION

UPWARD: What did God teach you about Himself through Galatians 5?

INWARD: How would your life change if you believed this truth?

OUTWARD: Share what you learned this week with a friend or family member.

CLOSE IN PRAYER

Thank God for being present with you in your study time and ask Him to help you live out the truth you learned this week in Galatians 5.

DISCUSS

Discuss the following questions with your Bible study group. A more extensive leader guide is available for free download at **lifeway.com/livefree**.

1. (Question 5, p. 134) How is our faith in Christ displayed in our lives (5:6)?

   (Question 6, p. 134) **REFLECT & RESPOND:** In what way do we as Christians elevate our religious practices over love for others? Give a few examples.

2. (Question 10, p. 136) What is the ultimate goal of our freedom? What happens if we lose sight of this goal (5:14-15)?

   (Question 12, p. 137) **REFLECT & RESPOND:** How does the world's definition of freedom differ from the freedom we have in Christ? When faced with the temptation to prioritize your personal desires over what glorifies God, how can you resist?

3. (Question 14, p. 140) Why is there a battle between the Spirit and our flesh (5:17-18)?

(Question 15, p. 141) **REFLECT & RESPOND:** What biblical encouragement can we hold onto when we experience this battle in our lives? Look up 1 Corinthians 10:13 and Philippians 2:13 and note what you learn.

4. (Question 22, p. 144) Discuss each aspect of the fruit of the Spirit and its opposite from the chart you filled out on page 144.

(Question 24, p. 145) **REFLECT & RESPOND:** How do you see the fruit of the Spirit growing in your life? What does it look like for you to "keep in step with the Spirit"?

5. (p. 146) **REFLECTION:**

Upward: What did God teach you about Himself through Galatians 5?

Inward: How would your life change if you believed this truth?

Outward: How can you share what you learned this week with a friend or family member?

WATCH

Watch the Session Seven video and take notes below.

TO ACCESS THE VIDEO SESSIONS, USE THE INSTRUCTIONS
IN THE BACK OF YOUR BIBLE STUDY BOOK.

149

Live
FREE

GALATIANS 6

When we stop trying to live on our own terms or striving to achieve God's favor, we will experience tremendous freedom. The blessing and goodness we all hope for only comes through God's grace. But to experience this grace, we have to relinquish our personal desires and submit to the way of Christ. Through each chapter in Galatians, Paul drives home this truth. He wants the Galatians to know that their false teachers are leading them towards being re-enslaved to the sin Christ gave His life to set them free from. In this last chapter, Paul gives one final warning and a word of encouragement to reaffirm the Judaizers' hypocrisy and the authenticity of his words. He will then end the book by highlighting the one thing we all need to remember to LIVE FREE.

Day One

CARRY ONE ANOTHER'S BURDENS (6:1-5)

We usually begin each week by reading through the entire book of Galatians. But since this is our last week of homework, we will start by digging into chapter 6—we'll read through the book as a part of our study wrap-up later this week! At the start of chapter 6, Paul emphasizes how our freedom in Christ should produce an overflow of love, leading us to help fellow believers overcome sin while we humbly take responsibility for our own actions.

> ¹ Brothers and sisters, if someone is overtaken in any wrongdoing, you who are spiritual, restore such a person with a gentle spirit, watching out for yourselves so that you also won't be tempted. ² Carry one another's burdens; in this way you will fulfill the law of Christ. ³ For if anyone considers himself to be something when he is nothing, he deceives himself. ⁴ Let each person examine his own work, and then he can take pride in himself alone, and not compare himself with someone else. ⁵ For each person will have to carry his own load.
>
> ―――――――――
>
> GALATIANS 6:1-5

1. What is the goal of restoring a person "overtaken in any wrongdoing" (6:1)? Read 1 Corinthians 1:10 for help with your answer.

   What would be the opposite of doing this in a gentle way?

2. What temptation(s) might we face as we try to help someone caught in sin (**6:1**)?

3. **REFLECT & RESPOND:** In order for us to carry one another's burdens we must be willing to ask for help or give help to a brother or sister in need. What are some things that hinder us from doing this? Which ones do you struggle with?

   How would the church be different if we did a better job of emulating Paul's words in **6:2**?

4. What is "the law of Christ" (**6:2**)? Read John 13:34 for help with your answer.

5. What type of comparison does Paul discourage in **6:3-4**? Explain why.

6. What is the difference between carrying one another's burdens and carrying our own load (**6:5**)?

7. **REFLECT & RESPOND:** Who has helped you carry your burdens? Write a prayer of gratitude for them below. Then, share your gratitude with them sometime this week.

Day Two

SOWING & REAPING (6:6-10)

We have to remember that every action we take has consequences. When we choose to live free in Christ, we sow seeds that will bring about a spiritual harvest of life and blessings. However, if we allow ourselves to become enslaved to our sinful desires, we will sow seeds that will produce a harvest of death and decay.

> [6] Let the one who is taught the word share all his good things with the teacher.
> [7] Don't be deceived: God is not mocked. For whatever a person sows he will also reap,
> [8] because the one who sows to his flesh will reap destruction from the flesh, but the one who sows to the Spirit will reap eternal life from the Spirit. [9] Let us not get tired of doing good, for we will reap at the proper time if we don't give up. [10] Therefore, as we have opportunity, let us work for the good of all, especially for those who belong to the household of faith.
>
> ———————
>
> GALATIANS 6:6-10

8. In **6:6**, what does Paul want the Galatians to share with the teacher? Read Philippians 4:14-18 for help with your answer.

9. Look up the word *mock* in a dictionary, and write a definition for it that best fits the way it is used in **6:7**.

MOCK

How does this definition help clarify your understanding of this verse?

10. Read Galatians **6:8** in the NIV and then answer the questions below.

    If we sow to please the flesh, what will we reap?

    If we sow to please the Spirit, what will we reap?

11. Does God's grace and forgiveness contradict what Paul is saying in **6:7-9**? Why or why not? Read Hebrews 12:5-6 for help with your answer.

12. **REFLECT & RESPOND:** What are some things that cause you to become weary as you have served others (**6:9**)? Give a few examples.

13. What can we do to persevere in our efforts to please the Spirit (**6:9-10**)?

14. **REFLECT & RESPOND:** Think about one or two people who belong to your household of faith (**6:10**). What is one practical way you can serve them this week? Share your response with the group and then follow up to share about your experience.

Therefore, as we have opportunity, let us work for the good of all, especially for those who belong to the household of faith.

Galatians 6:10

FINAL WORDS (6:11-18)

Paul provides his final words of encouragement, which includes one last reminder about the hypocrisy of the Judaizers and his faithful commitment to the truth. He ends the letter by focusing the Galatians on what really matters, their corporate transformation into a new creation in Christ.

> [11] Look at what large letters I use as I write to you in my own handwriting. [12] Those who want to make a good impression in the flesh are the ones who would compel you to be circumcised—but only to avoid being persecuted for the cross of Christ. [13] For even the circumcised don't keep the law themselves, and yet they want you to be circumcised in order to boast about your flesh. [14] But as for me, I will never boast about anything except the cross of our Lord Jesus Christ. The world has been crucified to me through the cross, and I to the world. [15] For both circumcision and uncircumcision mean nothing; what matters instead is a new creation. [16] May peace come to all those who follow this standard, and mercy even to the Israel of God! [17] From now on, let no one cause me trouble, because I bear on my body the marks of Jesus. [18] Brothers and sisters, the grace of our Lord Jesus Christ be with your spirit. Amen.
>
> ———————
>
> GALATIANS 6:11-18

15. What does the size of Paul's handwriting communicate to the Galatians (**6:11**)?

16. How are the actions of the Judaizers (**6:12-13**) similar to the actions of Peter in **2:11-14**?

    How do they differ from the actions of Paul (**6:14**)?

17. Read Galatians **6:15** in the NLT. What matters more than circumcision? Explain why.

18. Read 2 Corinthians 11:23-25. What does Paul mean by "marks of Jesus" (**6:17**)?

19. Read **6:15-18** again. According to Paul, how will the Galatians experience the peace, mercy, and grace of God?

For more, read "Let's Talk About: Being a New Creation" (p. 160).

What do these verses communicate about Paul's hope for the Galatians?

20. **REFLECT & RESPOND:** Take a moment to reflect on Paul's final words in **6:15-18**. Based on Paul's words, how can you experience the peace, mercy, and grace of God?

LET'S TALK ABOUT

Being a New Creation

Galatians 6:15

At the end of the book of Galatians, Paul provides one verse that helps summarize the main idea of his entire letter. In Galatians 6:15, Paul says, "both circumcision and uncircumcision mean nothing; what matters instead is a new creation." For most of the letter, Paul has been defending why circumcision is not necessary for salvation, and as a capstone to his argument he tells them their focus should instead be on their identity as a new creation.

Paul uses this same language in 2 Corinthians 5:17, when he talks about the transformation symbolized through our baptism in Christ. We have died to sin and been raised to new life, reborn to live as new people. This spiritual rebirth forms the foundation for our identity and characterizes our actions. Like Paul said in Galatians 2:20, we have been crucified with Christ, and it is no longer we who live but Christ who lives in us.

What is notable about Paul's use of the phrase "new creation" is that its meaning has both individual and corporate implications. I appreciate how Scot McKnight describes this literary element:

> While it is certainly wrong to exclude the individual from this principle, narrowing it to an individual is inaccurate. What Paul is doing here is contrasting two systems, the circumcision system of Moses and the uncircumcision system of the Gentile world. He insists it does not matter whether you are Jew or Gentile; what matters now is that there is no national circle into which one must enter to join the people of God. What matters is that you are part of God's new people, God's new creation, God's new humanity. [1]

The Galatians were a community of people who struggled with issues of division. As we saw in chapter 2, the false teaching of the Judaizers was leading to the mistreatment of the Gentiles. So, while Paul was adamant about correcting their false doctrine, he wasn't doing it to only give them personal assurance of salvation by faith. Paul knew that false doctrine could lead to sinful behavior. His letter of theological correction was designed to refocus the Galatians on that which really mattered— their unified identity and mission as the people of God.

Like Paul said in Galatians 2:20, we have been crucified with Christ, and it is no longer we who live but Christ who lives in us.

REFLECTION

UPWARD: What did God teach you about Himself through Galatians 6?

INWARD: How would your life change if you believed this truth?

OUTWARD: Share what you learned this week with a friend or family member.

CLOSE IN PRAYER

Thank God for being present with you in your study time and ask Him to help you live out the truth you learned this week in Galatians 6.

Day Four

FINAL READING DAY!

We are going to finish our study of Galatians by reading through the book one last time! As you read, write down any fresh observations or questions that pop up.

How has reading through Galatians multiple times over the past few weeks impacted your understanding of this book?

How did the process of repetitive reading answer any questions that popped up in the first few weeks of the study?

Day Five

STUDY WRAP-UP

To wrap up this study, we are going to take a few moments to review what we've learned. The goal of our study of the Bible is to grow in our knowledge and love for God, which then impacts how we love ourselves and love others. As you briefly review each week's lesson, take time to consider how studying Galatians has helped you do these things.

> Review your wrap-up questions from each session and then, in the table below, note the attribute(s) of God that stood out to you from that part of Galatians. A list of God's attributes can be found on pages 170-171.

	ATTRIBUTE OF GOD
Session Two (1:1-24)	
Session Three (2:1-21)	
Session Four (3:1-14)	
Session Five (3:15–4:7)	
Session Six (4:8-31)	
Session Seven (5:1-26)	
Session Eight (6:1-18)	

How has the book of Galatians transformed your view of God?

How has it transformed your understanding of who you're called to be as an image bearer?

What are your three main takeaways from this study? How will they help you LIVE FREE?

KEY TAKEAWAY	ONE WAY YOU WILL APPLY IT

Write a prayer below, thanking God for what you've learned and asking Him to help you live it out.

DISCUSS

Discuss the following questions with your Bible study group. A more extensive leader guide is available for free download at **lifeway.com/livefree**.

1. (Question 2, p. 153) What temptation(s) might we face as we try to help someone caught in sin (6:1)?

    (Question 3, p. 153) **REFLECT & RESPOND:** In order for us to carry one another's burdens we must be willing to ask for help or give help to a brother or sister in need. What are some things that hinder us from doing this? Which ones do you struggle with? How would the church be different if we did a better job of emulating Paul's words in 6:2?

2. (Question 13, p. 156) What can we do to persevere in our efforts to please the Spirit (6:9-10)?

    (Question 14, p. 156) **REFLECT & RESPOND:** Think about one or two people who belong to your household of faith (6:10). What is one practical way you can serve them this week? Share your response with the group and then follow up to share about your experience.

3. (Question 19, p. 159) Read 6:15-18 again. According to Paul, how will the Galatians experience the peace, mercy, and grace of God? What do these verses communicate about Paul's hope for the Galatians?

    (Question 20, p. 159) **REFLECT & RESPOND:** Take a moment to reflect on Paul's final words in 6:15-18. Based on Paul's words, how can you experience the peace, mercy, and grace of God?

4. (p. 165) How has the book of Galatians transformed your view of God? How has it transformed your understanding of who you're called to be as an image bearer?

5. (p. 166) What are your three main takeaways from this study? How will they help you LIVE FREE?

WATCH

Watch the Session Eight video and take notes below.

TO ACCESS THE VIDEO SESSIONS, USE THE INSTRUCTIONS
IN THE BACK OF YOUR BIBLE STUDY BOOK.

169

Attributes of God

Attentive: God hears and responds to the needs of His children.

Compassionate: God cares for His children and acts on their behalf.

Creator: God made everything. He is uncreated.

Deliverer: God rescues and saves His children.

Eternal: God is not limited by time; He exists outside of time.

Faithful: God always keeps His promises.

Generous: God gives what is best and beyond what is deserved.

Glorious: God displays His greatness and worth.

Good: God is what is best and gives what is best. He is incapable of doing harm.

Holy: God is perfect, pure, and without sin.

Immutable/Unchanging: God never changes. He is the same yesterday, today, and tomorrow.

Incomprehensible: God is beyond our understanding. We can comprehend Him in part but not in whole.

Infinite: God has no limits in His person or on His power.

Jealous: God will not share His glory with another. All glory rightfully belongs to Him.

Just: God is fair in all His actions and judgments. He cannot over-punish or under-punish.

Loving: God feels and displays infinite, unconditional affection toward His children. His love for them does not depend on their worth, response, or merit.

Merciful: God does not give His children the punishment they deserve.

Omnipotent/Almighty: God holds all power. Nothing is too hard for God. What He wills He can accomplish.

Omnipresent: God is fully present everywhere.

Omniscient: God knows everything, past, present, and future—all potential and real outcomes, all things micro and macro.

Patient/Long-suffering: God is untiring and bears with His children.

Provider: God meets the needs of His children.

Refuge: God is a place of safety and protection for His children.

Righteous: God is always good and right.

Self-existent: God depends on nothing and no one to give Him life or existence.

Self-sufficient: God is not vulnerable. He has no needs.

Sovereign: God does everything according to His plan and pleasure. He controls all things.

Transcendent: God is not like humans. He is infinitely higher in being and action.

Truthful: Whatever God speaks or does is truth and reality.

Wise: God knows what is best and acts accordingly. He cannot choose wrongly.

Worthy: God deserves all glory and honor and praise.

Wrathful: God hates all unrighteousness.

ENDNOTES

FOREWORD

1. Two books that can help you learn more about this study method are: *How to Read the Bible for All It's Worth* by Gordon Fee and *Women of the Word* by Jen Wilkin.

SESSION ONE

1. These dates are compiled from the following sources:

   The NIV Biblical Theology Study Bible: Follow God's Redemptive Plan as It Unfolds Throughout Scripture (United Kingdom: Zondervan, 2018), 1976.

   D. R. W. Wood, "Chronology of the Apostolic Age," *New Bible Dictionary* (United Kingdom: InterVarsity Press, 1996).

   "Major Events in the Life of the Apostle Paul," ESV.com, accessed September 9, 2024, https://www.esv.org/resources/esv-global-study-bible/chart-44-06/.

2. Thomas V. Brisco, "Map 119," *Holman Bible Atlas: A Complete Guide to the Expansive Geography of Biblical History*, (United States: B&H Publishing Group, 2014), 245.

SESSION TWO

1. Timothy Keller, *Galatians for You: For Reading, for Feeding, for Leading* (United Kingdom: Good Book Company, 2013), 10.
   David Witthoff, ed., *The Lexham Cultural Ontology Glossary* (Bellingham, WA: Lexham Press, 2014).

2. "On one end of the spectrum translators will choose to translate the Bible as strictly as the words and the grammar of the original language dictates. This is often called "formal equivalence" or word-for-word translation. . . . On the other end of the spectrum, translators will work to make sure the concepts and ideas of the original writers are brought about in the translation, rather than trying to force the exact words. This philosophy is called 'dynamic equivalence,' or thought-for-thought translation."
   Brandon D. Smith and Jeremy Writebol, "Why All The Translations?," Lifeway.com, accessed 10.28.2024, https://www.lifeway.com/en/special-emphasis/read-the-bible/articles/why-all-the-translations.

3. Scot McKnight, *Galatians*, The NIV Application Commentary (Grand Rapids, MI: Zondervan Publishing House, 1995), 51.

4. Gail R. O'Day, "Glad Tidings," *The Anchor Yale Bible Dictionary*, David Noel Freedman ed. (New York: Doubleday, 1992), 1031.

5. Nijay K. Gupta, *The Story of God Commentary - Galatians* (Zondervan Academic, 2024) 43-44.

SESSION THREE

1. "In Gal 2 Paul told of a conference in Jerusalem that had many similarities to Acts 15:1–35. Although the two accounts contain significant differences, the similarities seem to outweigh these, and it is probable that they relate to the same event."
   John B. Polhill, *Acts*, vol. 26, The New American Commentary (Nashville: Broadman & Holman Publishers, 1992), 321.

2. Patrick Schreiner, *The Kingdom of God and The Glory of the Cross* (Wheaton, IL: Crossway, 2018), 38.

SESSION FOUR

1. Tony Evans, *Kingdom Prayer* (Moody Publishers: Chicago, 2016), 121.

2. R. Alan Cole, *Galatians: An Introduction and Commentary*, vol. 9, Tyndale New Testament Commentaries (Downers Grove, IL: InterVarsity Press, 1989), 139.

SESSION FIVE

1. Cole, 147.

2. Jen Wilkin, "Applying the Books of the Law," LifewayWomen, February 21, 2018, https://women.lifeway.com/2018/02/21/reference-desk-applying-the-books-of-law/.

3. Scot McKnight, *The NIV Application Commentary: Galatians* (Zondervan Academic, 1995).

4. John Stott, *The Message of Galatians: Only One Way*, The Bible Speaks Today (Leicester, England; Downer's Grove, IL: InterVarsity Press, 1986), 97.

SESSION SIX

1. Michelle J. Morris, "Sarah," ed. John D. Barry et al., *The Lexham Bible Dictionary* (Bellingham, WA: Lexham Press, 2016).

2. Larry L. Walker, Elmer A. Martens, *Cornerstone Biblical Commentary: Isaiah, Jeremiah, & Lamentations*, vol. 8 (Carol Stream, IL: Tyndale House Publishers, 2005), 239.

SESSION SEVEN

1. J.I. Packer, *Rediscovering Holiness: Know the Fullness of Life with God* (United States: Gospel Light, 2009), 86.

2. Packer, 27.

SESSION EIGHT

1. McKnight, 302.

The entire story of Scripture helps us know who God is, who we are, and what we are called to do in His world.

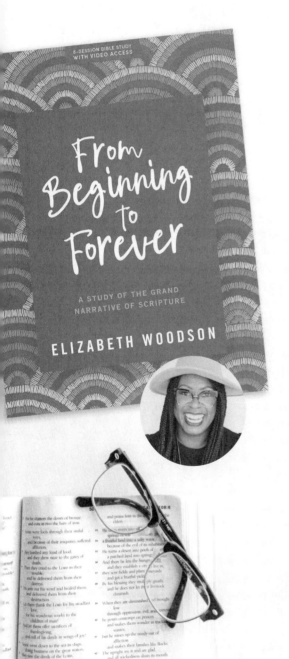

The size and scope of Scripture can be intimidating and overwhelming. And often we view it through the lens of our individual stories, looking for different verses or passages to help us live our everyday lives. But, in our search for personal truth, we fail to see how the entirety of Scripture works together to show a bigger story—God's redemption and restoration of the entire world.

In this 8-session study, Elizabeth Woodson introduces you to this story, showing how all 66 books of the Bible come together to form one unified narrative. Through the rich theological truths found in Genesis through Revelation, we'll see the eternal significance of what God is doing in the world and how He invites us to be a part of it.

Bible Study Book with Video Access
005837658 **$21.99**

lifeway.com/forever

Lifeway women

also available from
ELIZABETH WOODSON

EMBRACE YOUR LIFE

HOW TO FIND JOY WHEN THE LIFE YOU
HAVE IS NOT THE LIFE YOU HOPED FOR

ELIZABETH WOODSON

B&H
PUBLISHING

Lifeway women
ACADEMY

Online courses for women, by women.

Are you curious about how to study the Bible more deeply and apply it to your daily life? Lifeway Women Academy offers courses on topics like practical ministry, historical and cultural context, and theology, to help you grow in your understanding of God's Word and gain confidence in sharing it with others.

If you're interested in learning how to study and teach the Bible on your own, how to make disciples at home and everywhere you go, and how you can use your gifts for the kingdom, Lifeway Women Academy is where you begin.

WITH LIFEWAY WOMEN ACADEMY, YOU WILL:

- Get on-demand courses you can complete at your own pace.
- Grow in your understanding of what the Bible says and how to study it faithfully.
- Gain confidence and competence in studying God's Word and leading others to do the same.
- Be equipped with knowledge and practical steps to love God and make disciples.

Learn from trusted teachers like:
Jen Wilkin, Elizabeth Woodson, and **Courtney Doctor**

DISCOVER
AVAILABLE COURSES

Get the most from your study.

Customize your Bible study time with a guided experience.

In this study you'll:

- Grow in your understanding of the gospel and how it changes you

- Walk verse-by-verse through the book of Galatians as you uncover all the truth it holds for you today

- Recognize the false gospels you are believing in and how the true gospel of Jesus Christ sets us free

- Come away with a renewed sense of the unity and belonging we have in Christ

STUDYING ON YOUR OWN?

Watch Elizabeth Woodson's teaching sessions, available via redemption code for individual video-streaming access, printed in this Bible study book.

LEADING A GROUP?

Each group member will need a *Live Free* Bible study book, which includes video access. Because all participants will have access to the video content, you can choose to watch the videos outside of your group meeting if desired. Or, if you're watching together and someone misses a group meeting, they'll have the flexibility to catch up! A DVD set is also available to purchase separately if desired.

DVD Set includes 8 video teaching sessions from Elizabeth Woodson, each approximately 30 minutes

eBook with video access, includes 8 video teaching sessions from Elizabeth Woodson, each approximately 30 minutes

Browse study formats, a free session sample, leader guide, video clips, church promotional materials, and more at

lifeway.com/livefree